#NotForTeens

The Next Generation's Prescription

#NotForTeens

The Next Generation's Prescription

ALYSE NEIBAUR

#NotForTeens: The Next Generation's Prescription

Copyright © 2020 by Alyse Neibaur

Author Photo by Camera Shy

Edited by Julie Swearingen (www.julieswearingen.com) @quailrun.co
Copy editing by Alison Cantrell @quailrun.co

Cover Design and Interior Typesetting by Melissa Williams Design

Video Cassette Copyright ©2020 graja, Adobe Stock; Label Sticker ©2020 Piman Khrutmuang, AdobeStock; Prescription papers ©2020 dolva, AdobeStock

ISBN: 978-0578728209

Published by Bottled Up Foundation, LLC bottledupfoundation.org; facebook.com/groups/bottledup and on Instagram @bottledupfoundation

Bottled Up Foundation logo designed by Erik Neibaur

Contact Alyse at authoralyseneibaur@gmail.com and www.bottledupfoundation.org

WARNING

It is now the year 2020, and this book is not being published under the same pretenses I had expected when planning the release of this book near the end of 2019. We are living in great turmoil with a pandemic raging across the globe, and racial injustices sweeping our nation. All people of all ages, races, gender, mental capacity... etc. are experiencing a great loss. Depression and anxiety are running rampant among the citizens of this globe. Our great nation is systemically broken, and there's no telling what changes are coming, who will be our next leaders, and what decisions we will have to make individually or collectively.

All this unknowing is causing a great amount of stress for all people. More so than I have ever witnessed in my lifetime. I had no idea what was about to befall our planet when I was writing this book with plans to reach out to children and families to talk about the hard things we live in like the opioid epidemic, abuse, bullying, other substance use, mental health, suicide prevention... etc in the year of 2020. And it is because of this that even I could not handle the amount of stress that fell onto my personal life. My own well being, along with that of my children, our family, and friends has all been in question.

How on earth do we take care of ourselves and each other in times like these?

For a moment I thought that maybe the release of a book like this would be more harmful and cause more problems than it would solve. I have a responsibility to share with you the topics I discuss in this book, the ones that will be hard to digest, and the emotions you'll feel if you relate to the words I've written. I do not want any harm to come to you, my dearest reader. You are important, your life is important. You have so much potential, more than anyone has ever told you before. You are beautiful, inside, and out. The love you have to give to the world and people around you is immense, and powerful, and you deserve the same love in return.

Support, and community have never been more important in our lives than in this very moment.

To you, my dearest reader, I share a word of warning before you read the text I've written and the experiences I've lived through.

You will read about the following:

*Drug use and addiction
*Abuse: emotional, physical, and sexual
*Mental health/illness
*Thoughts of suicide, and suicide itself
*Cutting and other personal infliction of injury
*Bullying and peer pressure

*Broken family dynamics

This book is meant to be for teenagers ranging in ages of 13-18, but there are many heavy topics that would require adult intervention should any topic come up as one that could cause emotional distress in the reader's life.

At the end of the book I outline a simple guide on how to create a support network, and how to reach out for that support. Please skip to that section at any point in your reading. It is there for you to give you the tools you need to have a whole and beautiful existence.

No matter your age, race, gender, sexual preferences... etc. you are wholly deserving of support, community, and love.

If you have no one else to turn to, you always have me. My email is authoralyseneibaur@gmail.com, and I promise you I check it regularly.

Read with caution.

I love you all,

Alyse Neibaur

Chapter 1

Sheltered

Hi, my name is Alyse, and I'm a Disney princess. *princess waves to the room and sits back down*

Room responds in chorus: "Hi, Alyse."

Yes, it's true. I'm a Disney princess. I like to wear tiaras, pink gowns, and sing at random to the animals in the forest behind my house. I am also obsessed with love and romance, and I'm still waiting for my happily ever after.

This was how I was raised. Aww, how cute! No wonder I'm so shy, sweet, and naive. *flutters eyelashes innocently*

I was raised on Disney movies.

Disney was my drug.

Still is.

#SorryNotSorry

Many in my generation suffer this same affliction. We can't help it—and Disney knows it. They're remaking all our old favorite princess movies into live-action, girl-powered crack. So that we may, now in our thirties and forties, relive the magic of daydreaming about having power in a world where we feel utterly powerless and give new hope to girls who had never seen the animated Princess Jasmine movie.

My mother used to record these movies for me on VHS.

"What's that?" you all shout. Let me google that real quick.

Google search bar: what does VHS stand for?

Google response: Video Home System.

Well, that didn't help at all. Do you know what film is? Like, actual film? Not just another word for movie, but the actual film rolls they used to record movies to? That's what a VHS was—a mini film roll that you could pop into a VCR and rewind or fast-forward to your favorite parts and sing and resing your favorite moments in your Disney princess movies. All these old-school VCRs had a record button, where you could pop in a blank VHS and record something broadcasting on television. You could also accidentally record over something like wedding videos or the birth of your little sister.

My mother would record videos for me that were safe for me to watch. Rated G or PG. Sometimes she would record my favorite cartoons so I could rewatch those again too, because we didn't have Netflix, Hulu, or Disney+ (you have no idea how long I've waited for this).

These blank VHS tapes came with labels to write down what you recorded. Mom would write "Aladdin, for Alyse" or "Cartoons, for Alyse." If it wasn't safe for me to watch, something a little more grown up or action packed for my big brother, Cody, who is ten years older than I am, she would write "not for Alyse" following the title of the movie or show she recorded. Once I got a bit older, she even got creative and started editing some movies to not include the sex or violence so that I could sit and laugh with my family as they watched the movie that was generally inappropriate for me to watch.

This is how my mother sheltered me.

For Alyse, and not for Alyse.

I believe that Mom screwed up by not realizing she had to shelter Cody until it was far too late. Ten years later, I come along and she thinks, "Hey, maybe I should try harder to keep some of these things away from such a young and fragile mind."

This is what my teens years boiled down to: For Alyse, and not for Alyse.

But it was never that easy. Once everything started happening, the lines blurred a lot. She did her best to shelter me, but she also really needed me. I needed to step up as one of the adults, so the adults around me gave me bits and pieces of what was happening while keeping the bigger picture out of reach. Without that bigger picture, though, I had to kind of create my own. I made assumptions. Some of it was accurate and some was not.

How much of your teen years do you feel like you're just kind of making up as you go along? Or just doing as you're told because all of the adults around you "said so!" or else?!

I want to quickly say that this is not a book about how to rebel against your parents or to tell you that your parents have it all wrong. Life doesn't actually change all that much once you go from your teen years to your adult years, and hopefully your parents really do have your best interest in mind, but, people, if you're reading this and you're thinking to yourself "my home life is broken" and you're sad, mad, anxious, stressed, lost, and confused, well, you sound a lot like I did.

I don't know what happened these past few generations of human beings, but as we've progressed as a race, we've started neglecting to give teenagers adequate information on how to handle their lives and make decisions. I'm not saying teens don't know how to make good decisions. I'm saying that teens don't know how to make any decisions. Sometimes you just land in the decision whether you made it or your parents did. That's a confusing mess to be in. How did you get there? I often found myself asking the same question.

"How did I get here?"

"Why does any of this matter?"

"What is my life really worth?"

I wish you didn't have to ask yourselves these questions, but inevitably you will. Who's to blame for that?

Your parents?

Society?

Your teachers?

You?

The correct answer is all the above, but focusing on who to blame doesn't work anymore. Our world is broken. Not just your home, guys, but your whole world is broken. Politics are broken. The climate is broken. Humanity is broken. There is no rewind on this mess that you've been thrown into, and I'm so terribly sorry for that.

If I could rewind my life and go back to when my family was a little more put together, I don't know if I would.

My family did make their own decisions, and they put me in a bad situation of abuse. That's on them, not on me, but what is on me is how I decided to deal with that. Now, that is a loaded statement you might hear from the adults in your life a lot. Dealing with that is not an easy task, which is why so many of us don't actually make it out of that abuse cycle. What is going to set you apart from them? What decisions will you make for yourself because, in the grand scheme of things, you are all that matters, and since the day you were born, you became a separate person with a separate life.

I'm going to write about a lot of hard things in this book, and if you find yourself relating, then I encourage you to seek help. I promise to help guide you on how to do that because this book is everything I didn't know I needed when I was a teenager and, wow, how different life would have been if someone had grabbed my hand, like I'm grabbing yours right now, and said, "You're going to be okay. I promise."

Chapter 2

No Fear

I've been playing a little game with the people I know. A game I will play with you right now. It's really simple: I'll say a word, and you say the first word that pops into your mind.

Here we go. The word is *teenager*.

.

.

.

What word did you come up with?

Here are some answers I've been given to that question: drama, angst, anxiety,

depression, anger, rebellion . . . etc.

Of all the answers I've been given for that question—and none of them were positive in nature—the first word I was given was *fear*.

Every word really says so much about the teenaged condition, and the word *fear*, I feel, really encapsulates all of it.

To be a teenager is to be afraid. Afraid of and for your future. Afraid of failing, with love or success in school or your future career. Afraid of what people think of you. Afraid of what YOU think of you. Afraid of disappointing your parents or yourself. Afraid of not living up to the potential you're supposed to have like the rest of society.

Since writing my book *Raised by Narcotics*, I've been asked this next question several times: "How did you get through it?"

How did I get through being a teenager? How did I survive and not become an addict? How did I become who I am today? To write words like this and hope to instill the same hope in other hopeless teens?

I dunno. ¯_(ツ)_/¯

But really, I do know, and this book is where I'm going to try very hard to put into words what happened. How I survived my teenage years in a broken, abusive, and drug-addicted household without fully knowing that's what I was living in.

Let's go back to the words above, though—the one's that describe being a teenager. As I said before, we have, like, a bazillion words in our language, and yet we have narrowed down the teenaged experience to a few really negative terms. No one hears the word *teenager* and goes, "Yeah, that was fun!"

Being a teenager is hard, even if you have everything you could ever hope to have. Who, as a teen, is thinking to themselves right now, "Yeah, I want to do this forever"? Probably someone, but I wouldn't know who.

Not only is being a teenager inherently depressing by nature, but it's also frowned upon by every surrounding generation. Older or younger, everyone in society is looking down their noses at teenagers. Sure, teens have opportunities for their futures, but teens don't understand the "real world." Everything you do as a teenager is to prepare for the inevitable "real world." As if your world is somehow fake. As if you're caught between your youthful make-believe games and the person you should be someday. You are not the person you should be, and everyone still looks at you like you're ten years old.

I have a secret, though. That make-believe world you're living in that everyone tells you that you will eventually grow out of one day—after you've finished high school or college or have even gone on to have a PhD and get to stick Doctor in front of your name— never actually changes. There's no shift into real-world responsibilities. In fact, I would believe that if that shift ever really happens, it is not, in fact, when you're in your early twenties, finishing college, and getting a taste of what your career will look like. No, that shift most likely happens when you're twelve. This is when the world changes. This is when the people you've known your entire life change too. They don't see you the same way anymore, and you don't see yourself the same way either. This is when you get your first real taste of decision-making. Picking which classes you might get to take in junior high or middle school. As you grow, you'll learn to drive, get your first job, and maybe find your first boyfriend or girlfriend (maybe one of each?). You'll discover what love means to you and what that might look like as you age and settle down or don't settle down. You'll pick the right education for whatever it is that brings you joy in life or decide to travel instead for a while and do freelance work. You could create your own business. Yeah, you can do that when you're thirteen. In fact, you can even start building your credit when you're really young. I wish I had known THAT piece of information . . .

Thanks for nothing, Moooomm!

Another useful tidbit is the ability to graduate high school with not only your diploma, but also your associate's degree.

The real world starts a lot sooner than any adult in your life is going to let on. The real world begins when you're just a cute, dweeby little tween with no clue what's really going on around you, and everything is going to suck. Like, a lot.

So you're a teenager, and the world sucks, and you're crammed with potential and no clear direction on how to be what you're supposed to be, or even who you want to be, and those two things almost never line up.

This is all terribly depressing, and unfortunately that's what being a teenager is. You have a weird almost freedom that only comes when you're a teen, and I think that despite all of the negative words we have associated with being a teenager, that would be why so many of us wish we could do it all over again, because THIS TIME we wouldn't take it for granted, and we would just have fun.

But maybe you're like me, and you just know there's no way in heaven or hell you would ever want to revisit those teen years again. The day you get out of those teen years will be the best day of your life, and you'll never look back. I know! Now that I'm in my thirties, nothing at all has changed. I would never go back. Being a teen was the single worst experience of my life, and I'm glad those years are over.

If you're living in that hell—and I'm sorry, parents, for swearing to your children—this book is for you. You are who I dedicate every breath I take each morning to, when I wake up and keep trying to face another day of my life and show people just like me and you, teens that feel hopeless, that there's a better life waiting for you. Maybe even right now and not when you finally turn eighteen and can move out on your own and be your own person. Trust me—I had those same dreams.

First, however, I want to share my own pain with you and show you just how not alone you are—even though you're feeling isolated and, quite honestly, let down by everyone around you.

You're a teenager, and you're living in fear, but you know what got me through being a teenager? That very same word, *fear*!

I was afraid of becoming one of them.

Chapter 3

Social Media Suicide

B ack in my day, social media didn't exist. Well, that's a lie. Myspace launched in 2003, when I was 17, but because we didn't own a computer, I was oblivious to it.

Facebook launched in 2004, Twitter in 2006, and Instagram in 2010. These days we have a myriad of social media options that it's almost too daunting to pick one and attempt to stick with it. Every friend has a different favorite app that they use, and because of this, we cram our smartphones, watches, or tablets with the various apps just to stay connected. I can't even recall a time in my life when everyone I knew was on only one of these websites or apps. What are the kids calling it these days? I'm starting to sound really old.

I am a little old now. Mid-thirties and trying to write a book that teenagers can relate to because, as your parents have said a million times to you before, "I was a teenager once" (as if you're going to believe that was ever true).

My point isn't *when* social media happened; it's that it did happen and that I believe I was actually the lucky one who didn't have to deal with that noise on top of everything else a teenager has to deal with. For me, it was much easier to hide. To be invisible. I was the shy, quiet girl who didn't really talk to anyone. I just floated from one friend group to another, never having any meaningful conversations and trying to keep to myself while still trying to have "friends." Looking back, those "friends" were just as much friends to me then as any of the friends I have on social media are today. Which is to say, those friendships were lacking in many ways. Being able to know of a lot of people, without actually knowing any of them at all.

I often wonder what life would have looked like if I had struggled the way that I did, in the family that I had, and could also turn to social media for any number of reasons. Such as to vent about a current situation—the way my mother was treating me perhaps? Maybe to try to friend a specific boy who I liked and hope that he didn't block me, which he almost certainly would have because I was not anyone's first choice. I was terribly awkward, overweight, and shy and had the worst acne imaginable. Not to mention having no fashion sense. Hand-me-downs from your mother, who shopped at the thrift store, did not even come close to being fashionable. Would I have been an easier target for people who thought I was a loner? A follower? Would I have posted my angsty poetry online to see if anyone was listening or cared and realized that, in fact, no, no one was listening or caring about my words? Would I fall into a deeper depression because I would try to be heard, but nothing would come of it? Would I have taken that as a sign that my life was pointless and . . . and what? Kill myself? Yeah, that's what I was going to say, but it's hard to say. I had wanted to despite the lack of social media, but how much easier would it have been to justify in the sea of people grazing across the land of the internet and realizing that none of them cared about my struggles? I wouldn't have seen that it wasn't because they didn't care. How could they know or understand the severity of it all? One or two angsty poems do not provide enough evidence for a broken and abusive household.

Let's flip this, though. What if I had social media throughout those hard times and had been brave enough to send a simple message to a neighbor or a friend, or, hey, the police department? I've certainly felt more capable of communicating via text, email, words on a screen or device than I ever have in person. Did I keep to myself because I didn't have another option of reaching out? But I had ink and paper and envelopes and stamps, so what about sending a letter? Would anyone have taken me seriously in that case? What about handing a letter to a teacher on my way out of one class and into the next? Putting the ball in their court, so to speak, and hoping they cared enough to reach out after reading my words and help me find solutions to my problems or at least guide me to a friendly listening ear.

Honestly, these are things I never thought about. It took me turning thirty before I finally saw a therapist for the first time. How could I have known as a teenager that these simple steps existed? How could I have known that I was even in a bad situation? Isn't everyone's family a little broken?

Say you actually tell someone—then what? What exactly can they do for you? You're still stuck, right? You can't just move out; your life isn't even really yours yet. Not until you're eighteen at least. You have to be and do what your parents tell you to be and do, and should you say something, you may actually end up making your own situation even worse. So you ask yourself, "Can I deal with things the way they are now?" The answer to that will always be yes. Because it is human nature to be resilient and to adapt. If children in developing countries can adapt to war and watching their friends and neighbors die on a daily basis, you can deal with your life too. That's not only what you find yourself saying in your own mind, but also what it means to be human. We adapt to our circumstances, and sometimes we thrive, and sometimes we don't.

We build a comfort zone. In the abuse that we deal with daily, we actually build habits to protect ourselves. By reaching out, even once, we throw ourselves out of that comfort zone, and it is unknown for how long we will be out of it. That is terrifying. So we stay because that is the easiest path to take. No matter how hard this path is, we already know it, and we know it well. That we know we can survive means that we aren't really that bad off, right?

I didn't recognize that I was being abused until it was all far too late, and they were all dead anyway, so now what?

Chapter 4

Raised by Narcotics

By the time I was twenty-five years old, I had lost three very important people: my aunt Teresa, my grandma Jane, and my mom, Diane. I was also married and had a little girl named Aryn (Teresa) and was pregnant with my son Nicolas (Dale). My aunt, grandma, and mom had died before I even knew if my second baby would be a boy or a girl. In fact, my last conversation with my mother had been telling her about the new baby over the phone and hearing how happy and excited she was for another grandchild. Not even a month later, she was gone.

My first book, *Raised by Narcotics*, explains everything. And this book is not necessarily a sequel or prequel to that book but a telling of what I went through in my teen years before they all died and, ultimately, what it was like growing up in that environment.

When I released that book in May 2019, I let my daughter read it. She was twelve at the time. Because she knows me, and my stories, I let her do this because these people are her family. These stories involve her mother, brother, and dad. She's mature for her age and a bookworm. She's a lot like me in her mannerisms, and I felt that she could handle it even though I knew that for her it would possibly be harder to read than for almost anyone else, outside of my brother, her uncle, Cody.

But I curse a lot, and there's some adult content that isn't something parents want their children reading. So I'm writing this book because I realized after publishing the first one that the people I really want to impact are teenagers. They're people like my daughter. They're you.

But you should be given a quick summary of the first book.

My family died as a direct result of the opioid epidemic. Something you may be familiar with personally, and for a teenager, that completely sucks. You might know people who have become addicted, overdosed, committed suicide, or become dealers thanks to their access to the medicine cabinet in any of their relatives' homes. You might even be one of these people.

I was one of these people.

That's why this book is so important. Because you get it, and (curse word) I really wish you didn't!

You need something to relate to, and I have just the story for you. The same story I wish I'd had when I was a teenager so that I could potentially feel less alone.

After you read this book, if your parents or guardians say it's okay, please read *Raised by Narcotics*. Or wait until you're old enough to do so, and then give it as a gift to your parents, if they're still around. (I don't know if it's really a gift-giving book, so maybe don't do that?) And that's an interesting statement for me to make. Sometimes people tell me about their parents and how they were addicts too, and my first question for them is, "Are they still alive?" Because mine are not. Well, my dad is, but he's a different story altogether. I've never met him in person (he's not even listed on my birth certificate). We don't talk. I can't assume to know whether he's a good guy or not. The short version of his story is that he had a son who was disabled years before he had me. He gave that son up for adoption, and when I came around, he left my mother before I was born. I know now that he later raised a third child with a woman he claimed was the love of his life. They raised that child together, and he played a huge part in raising the children she had from her previous marriage. He was a father, to someone, and maybe even a good one, but not to me.

This story isn't truly about him, though. In part, it is because I came from a broken home. Pieces missing, weird ones taking the places of those missing pieces, and some pieces so shattered that there's just no telling what on earth they were supposed to look like. That's life. That's family. That is the unfortunate truth in so many households right now.

Deadbeat dads. Deadbeat moms. I've seen it happen. Blended families, living with cousins or grandparents. Maybe you're part of the small percentage who had to be handed off to your godparents. Maybe you were adopted, but then your parents divorced. Maybe you live with your mom, but you really wish you lived with your dad. Maybe you have two dads or two moms or moms and dads who bring home several partners all the time.

I have an entire chapter in *Raised by Narcotics* called "Family." Ultimately, I ask, what does that word mean to you? Every single family looks different. Mine was me, Mom, Cody, and eventually Grandma Jane and Aunt Teresa. These were the people I shared a home with. When you share a home with someone, you must develop a certain level of both companionship and trust. They are literally living in your bubble, and there's nothing you can do about it.

For me, family means trust. Who do you trust in good times and in bad times? And that's important. I think it's easy to trust people when things are good, but what about when things are bad? And do they trust you? Are you someone they can count on? Do you count on them? It goes both ways.

Right before I turned twelve—the same age my girl was when she read these stories—my family was faced with some pretty massive decisions. We had to figure out what all of that meant, who we could count on, and who we couldn't, and even the smallest member of the family (me) had to step up and help. I should never have had to face that choice the way that I did, but family is family, right? Blood is thicker than water? If you believe that, I'm going to test it because I certainly do not. My mother was big on respecting your elders. If someone was older than you, you pay respect no matter their opinion. Mom was a boomer though, and boomers have a different logic about them. We don't live in that world anymore, and I was lucky enough to start questioning that logic when I was a teenager.

Family means trust, and my current family includes people who are not blood related and I would trust them with my life. That's family.

There are lines in this world, and despite being family, my mother crossed them. That's abuse. Because I was a child and didn't really have much of a choice, and if I did, well, I had no idea what my choices were, who I could trust, or where I could turn for answers to questions I didn't know I needed to ask.

They were all dead by the time I was twenty-five years old. I didn't realize it was abuse until I was thirty. Guys . . . don't be me. Open those eyes.

#OpenYourEyes

So what happened?

Chapter 5

Drugs, M'kay

Who has seen *South Park*? Yeah, I grew up on that show. I technically wasn't supposed to watch it (#NotForAlyse), but at a certain point in life, I think the adults around you have to give up a little bit, especially if your little teenaged self is taking care of them.

And by no means was I little. For all the chubby kids out there, I feel ya. I weighed nearly 170 pounds by the time I was thirteen. To put that into perspective, the average weight of a twelve-year-old girl is around ninety-two to one hundred pounds, with weight varying between seventy to 135 pounds for that age range depending on height and genetics. So, at that age, I was already about thirty pounds heavier than the top weight range and seventy pounds heavier than the average girl my same age. I don't want to say this to be disparaging or to make you look in the mirror and think you're fat or not beautiful. Our world has changed a lot, especially in relation to food. You are beautiful, and none of this matters. I learned years later as a health coach (that didn't last long) that teens should not be focused on losing weight but instead focused on growing and creating healthy habits. Your weight does not matter, just as mine did not, and does not. I say it to give you a clear picture of who I was and honestly still am.

My comfort foods were Cap'n Crunch's Peanut Butter Crunch, cheesy Doritos, and REESE'S Peanut Butter Cups. Alright?! Okay. I was addicted to junk food. I didn't know any other way to be.

So, as I sat watching a vulgar show that I probably wouldn't let my own kids watch at the same age I was watching it, I also had a bowl of Doritos in my lap. Possibly the entire bag, but let's move on.

One iconic moment in the early days of that now long-running show was the joke that "drugs are bad, m'kay." Good old Mr. Mackey. Ha ha ha.

Mom used to correct my incorrect language. I would say *m'kay* a lot, and she would say "Alyse, it's okay, not m'kay." To which I would reply . . . "m'kay."

M'kay.

South Park was released in 1997. Now I wasn't the only one saying *m'kay* because Mr. Mackey's little catchphrase caught on in my household. We were all laughing over this in a very sad way after the devastating car accident that Grandma and Teresa had been in.

I'm going to burn through this part quickly.

#KeepUp

They were involved in a car accident when I was eleven. Grandma was driving with Teresa in the passenger seat. They were headed to a mental health appointment for Teresa. My aunt was both bipolar and schizophrenic. Not something to take lightly, and it played a huge role in my life and in the accident that left her nearly paralyzed. A driver turning and going through an intersection had fallen asleep at the wheel and plowed into the passenger side of their car. Grandma Jane was lucky and walked away with minor injuries. Bumps, bruises . . . Teresa, on the other hand, was far less lucky. Her back was broken as her spine twisted in her seat upon impact.

They were right outside of a hospital, which is ultimately what saved her life. She was rushed to surgery, and family was called.

I was sitting in the living room of Grandma's house when that phone call came in. Probably eating my bowl of junk food and watching some random cartoon in my pajamas. I remember Mom's reaction, and then I remember sitting in a seat at the end of Teresa's hospital bed and watching the doctor tickle her toes to see if they would move.

They did. Just barely. Teresa would walk again, but it would take a large amount of painkillers, a walker, a special bed, and around-the-clock care by the rest of us. Our family was barely making ends meet. Trying to afford a rehab clinic or in-home nurse was out of the question.

We faced insurmountable decision-making back to back. Impossible decisions made for us, in a way. What else were we supposed to do? Let her die? Let her suffer? No, you don't do that. It's inhumane. That's awful.

I wish Teresa were here to tell you her story. What a crazy life she led. In a very real way, she was a sister to me.

Every year we shared a birthday because I was born three days before hers. So we combined our celebrations. She was a role model to me in what it meant to be human. She didn't like being a girl. She thought she was a boy in a woman's body, and she was a lesbian (she liked girls). She let me ask all kinds of questions in my little kid way and helped open my mind to things that would later affect my view of the world around me and help me be more tolerant and patient, with myself and with others. I want to quickly say here that your identity is a big deal. Don't ever let anyone mock you for being who you are. You are beautiful and wonderful. Period.

In addition to her bipolar disorder and schizophrenia, Teresa was an alcoholic. And then after the car accident, she required all kinds of painkillers and such to keep her, hmmm, not happy, but not in pain either. She was the first drug addict I would ever know. The ailments in her life were a very deadly combination.

Mental disorders, plus alcoholism, plus drug addiction . . .

Seriously, how did doctors not recognize that the only place that would lead was her eventual death?

And it did, but I'll get to that much later. We have six years to go before we get there, and all of them were my very fragile teenage years where life already didn't make sense, and my body was changing, my boobs were growing, and for the first time, I was trying to feel feminine (there really is a third book here solely on identity issues in this country—I am just one of many who have struggled with this), and then life just flipped on its head.

That accident was the catalyst for every single piece of trauma I experienced until I was twenty-five years old, maybe thirty. But who should I blame?

Chapter 6

Fitting In

Have you, during your teen years, considered what the financial climate might look like when you're an adult? Me either. What does *financial climate* even mean? And is it warming?

No, it's not warming; in fact, it's getting colder. The amount of debt that millennials—your parents (including me)—have is some ridiculous percentage higher than the previous generations (boomers and Gen X). Although my mom, a boomer, was a single mother, she was actually far richer than most millennial families are today. Having the ability to rent her own home, on the type of entry-level jobs she was able to hold down, is unheard of these days. Let alone putting her children into day care and paying for any kind of after-school activities, which she did. Mom felt incredibly poor, and she was. Living paycheck to paycheck, and as she put it "robbing Peter to pay Paul," meaning she took out loans to pay off other loans. For as long as I could remember, we always had debt. In fact, from a very early age, I remember sitting in a loan office and hearing that my mother needed to "sign a lease" and I thought they said "sign Alyse," and I had a tantrum because I didn't want anyone to sign me. So, if Mom were still around, she would still be the one making that joke and laughing about it to this day. I never heard the end of that one.

Mom, it wasn't funny. I thought they were going to sign me and sell me. I thought that was how loans worked, and I was devastated. M'kay?!

What I'm trying to say is that I, a millennial, am terrified for my Gen Z kiddos. Their financial future looks grim. That's your future too. It certainly feels as if you have to sell your soul just to have food and shelter these days.

I think we've forgotten how to human.

Being human is incredibly basic. We don't need very much to survive at all. Our current society has put in place some unreasonably high standards, and being human is almost a luxury these days. Having a life that you are content with, not happy with, not even remotely satisfied with, is something of a struggle for most people. This is the life you're preparing for! And it just kills me!

I could rant for ages about this. The scariest part about it is, that even though we know it's happening, we play into it. As we grow and become adults, we fall into the same lines, or, at least, most of us do. That means that we are helping to create some of the problems that are only getting worse with time.

Consider our nation.

Consider our finances.

Consider your education.

Consider the climate.

I grew up in the '90s where all of these things were difficult, and those things have only grown more difficult.

Society dictates that if you are not within a certain average mental state, or financial state, you won't make it.

My family didn't make it.

My aunt Teresa had two very serious mental illnesses. She was never able to hold down a job, and because of that, she lived her entire life with her mother, my grandma Jane.

Over the years, my mother's list of mental and physical problems grew and grew as well. She eventually became as dependent on Grandma Jane as Teresa, although I feel that it all could have been avoided.

This put a huge strain on my grandmother, who was now thrown backward into mothering her adult children, as well as her two grandchildren—me and my brother, Cody (who was eighteen when we moved in with her, an adult already). The older Cody got, the better off he was because at least he could work, earn his own income, and eventually move out. Largely he took care of himself, but because I was a good ten years younger, life was much different for me.

When I was nine, we moved in with Grandma Jane. At this point, I had to switch schools and began getting bullied by the popular girls at my new elementary school. They started asking me uncomfortable questions about my life: why I didn't have a dad, why I lived with my grandmother, did I hate it. When they noticed how shy I was, they started manipulating me and telling me to do certain things to other kids, and if I didn't, they wouldn't be my friends anymore. At that point, I decided, fine, don't be my friends anymore. It wasn't worth the turmoil to hurt other children. There was already a pain growing within me that I couldn't quite understand, and it just felt better to be alone. Of course, though, I started hating school because that loneliness I preferred provoked name-calling. I was called *loner* and then started having breakdowns and refusing to go to school. I refused so much that halfway through my fifth-grade year, Mom pulled me out of that school and put me back in my old one. My problem now was that my friends there had already moved on, and I had changed enough internally that I no longer fit in with them. I was now an afterthought. Oh, Alyse is back, but we don't really need her anymore, and so I stayed alone. At least there, they didn't bully me; they just didn't need me anymore, and I can't tell you which feeling is worse.

Suddenly I was just out of place.

My old home was being lived in by some strangers who had no idea how cherished my life was there, and because of them, everything I knew and loved was changing and getting worse.

Now I had to go home to a place where one of the adults could snap at any moment, and my mom and grandma fought so much over space and whether or not my mom should try to get a new place, I never knew if I was going to stay or go. My life wasn't stable, my friendships weren't stable, and I found myself questioning things in my life that I hadn't ever put much thought into, but now I wondered, "Why didn't my dad love me enough to stay and be my dad?"

I was ten years old, in fifth grade, and suffering from depression and thoughts that were starting to confuse me and make me really, really sad.

Just recently, now as we sit here at the end of 2019, I received an email from the principal of my son's school. One of the children at school had passed away, and the family was allowing the school to share the information. Before I read too much further, I thought, "Oh no, maybe cancer, maybe an accident of some kind, that's just awful." Once I kept reading, I saw the word *suicide*, followed by *fourth grader*. Oh. My. God.

A fourth-grade student at my son's school took their own life right before the holidays.

My first thoughts were how and why. How does a fourth grader even know what those feelings feel like? And why would they feel that desperate to end a life that had only just really started?

Of course, I began reflecting on my own experiences, and unfortunately, I started to get it. The difference today versus when I was in elementary school is what children now have more access to. They have access to a very adult world through many mediums, and not just that but everyone around them is depressed and stressed out. If even one person in this child's life had said the word *suicide* out loud, now it is stuck in this child's head, and that's all it takes.

How many things have I said out loud in front of my children thinking they're not listening? They're just watching TV . . . blah blah blah . . .

What are some things you remember from those elementary years?

Those were the years that made me break. I was full of childhood wonder, and happiness, and it all ended the summer before I entered fifth grade. No one put suicide into my head until I was much older, but if they had, would I have been one of those kids? I know how impressionable I was back then, and I did make some scary decisions because of what I saw on TV or what I heard within the walls of my home. And I want to be very clear here, I'm not saying it was because I saw some violence in a cartoon. The types of shows my mother watched were talk shows. People coming on the show and talking about real-life problems. Between that and the real-life problems I was facing, I was looking at these situations laid out in front of me and wondering how it all applied to my own life. I was comparing my life to everything I saw, or heard, around me. I was being given new perspectives, new ways of seeing things, and some were good, and others were bad. My bullies taught me to hate myself, and the situation I was living in was teaching me how to be angry.

What I wanted to know more than anything was how to fit in with my surroundings, when it felt like everyone just wanted me to either do their bad deeds for them or go away entirely.

Chapter 7

BFF

My best friend's name is Amanda Jane. She was named after our grandma Jane. She's the very best person in the entire world in my opinion. I hope we all have an Amanda Jane in our lives. If you have a best friend like her, don't let them go.

She and I are lucky enough to be cousins. Our mothers are sisters (first was Teresa, then came Diane, my mom, and then there was Sylvia, the youngest of the three girls), and they were pregnant with us at the same time. She was born one month before I was in the summer of 1986.

I mention her because, in many ways, I believe she kind of saved me from myself, and I know that feeling is mutual. We both grew up in the same family with slightly different problems. Her home was just as broken as mine, maybe even more so. I would hope one day she would write her story down as well because, wow, this woman is a strong female warrior who has faced all the adversity while simultaneously suffering from epilepsy in a home that couldn't afford for her to have epilepsy.

Her seizures scared the crap out of me, and I was always afraid of her dying. Who would I even be without Amanda Jane to stand next to me through the turmoil of our lives?! That is when I would truly be nothing.

She and I were treated like twins. Our moms would buy us the same outfits, and we spent every holiday and summer together. Nearly every photo I have from my childhood, she's there right next to me.

She's the very reason that I believe in support. Having even just one person to lean on in truly hard times, that can save a life. Multiple times, that can save the same life. She and I saved each other, and she is still my very best friend, sister, soul mate . . . you get it. I would die for her. She would die for me.

#BestFriendsForever

And now I'm trying to decide how this whole tangent on having a best friend ties into the rest of the story.

There was a moment when we were kids, watching our family get drunk together. Diane, Sylvia, and Teresa. Three sisters, doing adult things and having a crazy Saturday night while the kids played in the back room.

Teresa got so blackout drunk that she needed to be lifted off the ground. I was always bigger than Mandy, and so I was volunteered to help lift her off the floor while she drunkenly laughed at us. I don't know why people think the chubby kid is somehow stronger. The whole situation scared me and made me feel sad. Mandy took me into her room, and we sat in the space between her bed and the wall and made a pact together. We would never in our whole entire lives end up like them. We swore this to each other, and I made her write it down in a notebook so we could remember it forever and sign our names so it would be unbreakable.

We were seven.

Amanda Jane, I think we've done a fairly good job keeping our promise.

But I keep coming back to this thought: what would my life have been like, what would situations like that have looked like, without her there? She comforted me and made things better. What if you don't have a make-things-better buddy?

Most don't. I think the bond she and I have is rare. We weren't real sisters, so we were allowed the space to be ourselves without having to compare ourselves to one another and bicker over stupid things. We were closer than two friends from separate families and understood each other and the dynamics of our extended family in a way other best friends don't get a chance to see or be part of.

So, yes, I had her as this partner in crime, the person I called for everything, the person I spent all of my free time with, this person who understood my family when I said, "Hey, so this thing happened . . ." And she just instantly got it because that was so Teresa or so Diane. We laughed together, we cried together, we understood each other.

When I wrote *Raised by Narcotics*, however, and had her read it, there were things in there that she hadn't realized had happened. There were things she didn't know about. There were pains she didn't know I carried, and the same was true in reverse. She suddenly opened up to me about some of her traumas that she carried completely alone throughout our childhood, and when she told me, I wept. I cried for this person who I knew better than anyone else on this planet because despite how close we were, there wasn't a way to fully be there or know what the other had been through.

Life is a lonely journey.

I say this to tell you that no matter who you have in your life right now, you don't know their secrets, and they don't know yours.

There may still be things I don't know, but as we've grown into adults, I think we've become a little more transparent with one another. We didn't want to face another moment like that, so now we spill it.

When you're a child, though, you're driven by fear, and that fear allows you to keep everything tucked inside. If anyone knew everything, what would that do to your life? To your comfort zone?

Amanda Jane and I were abused. In different ways, and from different people, and we were both scared to let it all out. Even with each other.

The one person in the world I felt safest with, I still didn't allow my secrets, and neither did she.

If she didn't know, then certainly no one else did, but here's the thing: we all have these things in common, but if I can suppress some of these terrible things with even the one person in the world I was closest to, why on earth would I share it with anyone else?

Why would you?

Why would you want to share your pain with a stranger or your parents if you're not even going to tell your BFF? What would make you want to reach out to a teacher? To a police officer? To a counselor?

I think about the meetings I sit in on now, the ones about youth drug prevention. A lot of it is the same hopeful message we want to share with the youth, but none of it creates the connection we can make that allows enough of a safety net for anyone to feel comfortable sharing. And if you're not comfortable sharing, you're going to try to make up answers for yourself. You're going to make your own decisions, and those decisions will fall in line with the things you see happening around you.

I don't want to say monkey see, monkey do, but we do the things our parents do. We live by example. If they set that example, that's how we live. That's what we know. We don't know better, and that's not your fault, or my fault, it just is. The life you live is the only life you know. How can you know differently? You can't.

And maybe Amanda Jane and I were too close. Maybe had my BFF been from a family that wasn't my own, I could have seen a different example. I mean, sure, I had other friends, and I saw other ways of life, but I was too shy to get close to people. Too shy to share my family situation, and I certainly didn't want to jeopardize that family I lived in. Because my life was so unstable, I didn't want to go rocking that boat and sinking myself. At least I had a home. At least I had food in my stomach. Although there were times when we didn't. There were times when what we were eating for dinner was saltine crackers with butter spread across the top. And I cry as I write this because I remember that pain, and I know that some of you—maybe even most of you—know that pain too.

In an effort to keep ourselves safe, we keep ourselves alone and in pain.

Chapter 8

Let Me Educate You

I'm going to teach you about drugs in this chapter. In a way that your schools will never do. Take notes.

By the time I was eleven years old, my entire world, as I thought I had known it, flipped on its head.

We had moved in with Grandma Jane and Aunt Teresa two years previously. I now shared a bedroom with my mother so that Cody could have his own room, being the only boy in the house. Mom occasionally lost her temper because she didn't like the way things in life were working out. Despite this, though, she was my friend. I looked up to her for anything a growing girl could need. And that meant a lot of emotional reassurance as my body and life were changing. Mom was a rock in my life.

Teresa kept to herself for the most part. She took her daily medication to keep herself emotionally stable, and I rarely saw her lose control. In fact, she was one of my best friends, as I've said before, like a sister to me.

Grandma Jane worked at an explosives factory up the canyon. Yes, you heard me right. My grandma was the coolest person in the world. She made explosives for a living! And back in the '80s, she also flew planes for the Civil Air Patrol! Do grandmas get any cooler than that?! No, they do not. Mine was the coolest. Cody eventually joined her at the explosives plant.

And that's what my family looked like when the accident happened.

There was the car accident in the spring, right before I turned twelve.

I suppose I must thank the powers of the universe that Grandma Jane was the one to make it out of that with only bumps and bruises. If one of them had to go breaking their backs, having it happen to the main breadwinner in the house would have made this story quite a bit different.

Teresa was already on government aid because of her mental health and inability to work. That she was the one put in this situation . . . I'm not thankful by any stretch of the imagination, but in hard times, you must find the silver linings. I cannot imagine that situation flipped. I just can't, and I shudder to think about it.

I hate saying that Teresa might have been better off dead in that situation because her quality of life completely vanished. And what it ultimately did to our family? Would we have all been better off grieving the loss of a loved one instead of what came afterward?

I guess that's why I have chosen to write books. I can't think of their lives and deaths as having meant nothing. I can't let them just become another statistic for the opioid epidemic. People, our families, are becoming numbers, and those numbers aren't accurate.

While Teresa was in the hospital, she was prescribed all kinds of medication. The biggest one was Lortab, to help with the pain.

Let's have a quick medication lesson.

#KnowledgeIsPower

In the drug world, there are different classes of drugs that doctors can prescribe to us. First, over-the-counter, or OTC, drugs are medications you can buy without a prescription.

Here are some examples: TYLENOL (acetaminophen), Advil (ibuprofen), Bayer/Exedrin (aspirin), and Aleve (naproxen sodium).

You may have all of these in your medicine cabinet at home. Each is a different type of drug, but we know them all to take away pain or reduce fevers. What they have are different active ingredients. Within our bodies, they do things a little different than the next and have different reactions to other medications. This is the same for prescription drugs prescribed by your doctors. Depending on your lifestyle and how old you are or what other medications you already take, they can narrow it down and decide on one over another.

That brings us to our second class of medications: narcotics. A narcotic is a heavy medication that can also be addictive. Lortab is a narcotic, a combination of hydrocodone and acetaminophen. Vicodin, one you are probably more familiar with by name, is also a combination of hydrocodone and acetaminophen. Both are also considered opioids, or opiates.

Opioids and narcotics are two words that share the same meaning: pain medication that triggers opiate receptors and can become addictive and habit-forming.

Originally, opioids were made by collecting the seeds from a poppy flower and making opium. Today's opioids are synthetic and created in a lab. These include fentanyl (known by several different names), morphine, and oxycodone (used in the name brands OxyContin and ROXICODONE).

Morphine and fentanyl are often prescribed for their anesthetic properties and in end-of-life palliative care. Oxycodone was meant to be a better alternative for severe pain management. Percocet is another medication that combines oxycodone with acetaminophen.

More and more school curricula are changing to include information about opioids, but none that I've seen thus far include the names of any of the actual prescriptions you might encounter within your own family or home.

The medications inside my home were Lortab, Percocet, morphine, OxyContin, and fentanyl. I knew all these names by the time I was fifteen years old—except fentanyl because that's not the name brand. As an ingredient, it is so powerful that even a small dose can cause people to overdose.

So why do they insist on using it?

You are right to be terrified of that and have that question.

I did not learn the names of these drugs, or what they do, by sitting in a classroom. Nor did I learn their value in a classroom. There are no teachers in this world who are going to tell you that you can sell Oxy for thirty to fifty dollars per pill (except that while this book was in edits, I read an article about a teacher selling pills to the students in their school—WTF?). No, indeed, I learned that from my family as well. And I don't tell you the value of these drugs so that you'll put the book down and start drug dealing. Don't do that, please. I say it because it all leads to something much bigger. Pharmacies and doctors and drug manufacturers and insurance companies raised their prices and sent people who don't have that kind of money in directions like drug dealing or, even worse, doing street drugs like heroin. There are a lot of complicated rules around drugs, and those rules mean that sometimes people make bad decisions because, in the short term, it makes more sense and more money. Doctors are people too. I am not just talking about addicts.

But let's please continue.

Teresa originally came home with Lortab. Our family's very first opioid. When I was a kid, we called them narcotics. Since the discovery that they kill people, they are now being called by their scientific name: opioids. Thank you, society.

Humans have opioid receptors all throughout their bodies. From your head to your toes, pretty much. Think of these receptors as doors. When you're in pain, they open, allowing the opioid to go in and close the door. Over time, your body forgets how to close these doors on its own and relies on the opioids to close the doors for it. This is how addiction starts, and you can become addicted within a matter of days. Not even a full week.

It's very simple math here. Teresa came home from the hospital with a thirty-day prescription for Lortab, to be refilled multiple times. It's okay for you to assume that she quickly became a drug addict, but what other choice did she have in dealing with the severe pain after breaking her back?

In addition to those opioid doors opening and closing inside of our bodies, our bodies can become resistant to these opioids. So, instead of these doors closing after you take a pill, they might stay open just a little bit, leaving you in just a little bit of pain. Over time, they may not close at all. You'll then find yourself taking higher doses of the same pill or asking for something stronger to get those doors to close. Things like Percocet, OxyContin, and morphine.

Phew!

Congratulations, you now know more about drugs than your family does.

Lastly, we need to talk about naloxone (brand names include NARCAN and EVZIO), which is not to be confused with SUBOXONE. Naloxone is not an opioid. In fact, naloxone is the antidote to opioids. The cure. The reverse-this-scary-thing-I-just-did thing. The thing that you can get, if someone has it on hand, if you look like you're about to die and possibly reverse the overdose.

I will tell you what an overdose looks like, but not yet.

What is SUBOXONE? I've only just learned about this one recently myself. SUBOXONE is another brand name for a drug whose two main ingredients are opioids and naloxone. Meant to help those struggling with addiction. Can we all take a moment to face-palm together?

#FacePalm

My family never had naloxone (or SUBOXONE). It does save lives, however, so because it is necessary, if you know someone taking opioids, having this on hand is a must. I am not a fan of any of these products. The ones that kill and the ones that either aid in recovery or during an actual overdose. All these products are meant to be sold to your families, friends, and you. The people who market each of these products want one thing: your money. The makers of the drug SUBOX-ONE are also the makers of the opioids that resulted in the deaths of hundreds of thousands of people over the years. The very same people making a quick buck on these addictions and overdoses are the ones selling the "cure" to addiction and overdose.

Let us face-palm one last time.

#FacePalm

Take a deep breath. I'm here for you.

It is hard to consume all that information, and I promise the rest of the book won't be like that. Consider this backstory, though. You need this information to understand the rest of the story and how it all connects to your own life. I want you to see the pieces of your life now and not when you're in your thirties looking back and going "oooohh . . . sh** . . ." like I did.

Don't be like Alyse.

#DontBeLikeAlyse

We all know that my family dies in the end. Except Cody. Thank goodness my big brother is still here; I don't know what I would do without him.

It is in how they each die that I feel this story is incredibly important. And how I lived with them before they each died. Because if you experience any of this, you probably need support and to talk to someone.

My entire goal is to help you understand that what you're living in isn't normal and should never become normal. We need to change this new normal, where our parents and our friends are dying over pills. That's not the life any of us want!

Chapter 9

Caretaker

Now that you know all about the pills that entered my home, let me tell you what my role in this family became.

As I was about to turn twelve, my family needed me to step up in a big way. I needed to leave my childhood behind me and take a part in nursing my aunt Teresa back to what would become her new normal. She could hardly walk; in fact, she could hardly bear her own weight. She needed a walker just to stand up.

There had been some discussion over our options to have her in a rehab facility or hire a nurse to come in and take care of her during the day, but these conversations were very short lived. We simply didn't have the money for any of it, and now even worse than not having the money to pay for it, we were in incredible medical debt from all her growing needs.

Thousands of dollars listed out on pieces of paper for every little thing that had occurred immediately following the accident, including the walker she would use and the hospital bed that would quickly replace the bed she slept in before she came home so that she could keep herself propped up at a less painful angle.

Some things were covered by the government assistance she was already on for being disabled with two serious mental illnesses, but, of course, they didn't cover everything.

Her bedroom was in the basement of the house. Getting her home and down the stairs was excruciating and slow. I stood behind her, Mom in front in case she fell forward, and Grandma holding her arm standing next to her as we very slowly got her one foot at a time down those thirteen steps. This was not just where her bedroom was, but where she lived. This was where she spent all her waking hours, but again, there was a long, drawn-out conversation about potentially changing it before she got home. Obviously, we chose not to because Grandma Jane wouldn't allow her to smoke upstairs. That was her good living room and where Mom and I lived, pretty much. It seriously was her smoking habit that clinched the deal on that. So we got her down those steps—I did practically nothing—but as she hobbled and moaned down the stairs, my life was changing right in front of my eyes. This was our new normal. Teresa was home, and we needed to take care of her, and as it turned out, the state of Utah would pay me, once I turned twelve years old, to be an in-home nurse for my aunt. In the few months before I turned twelve, Mom taught me everything I needed to know in how to care for my newly disabled aunt.

I became a caretaker, and this role would define who I am for the rest of my life.

My twelfth birthday was bittersweet. There were papers to sign so that I could officially "work" from home, a concept I didn't really understand. I was given a few jobs, and Mom showed me how to do everything, even if it wasn't included in my new position.

Mom was an assistant at retirement homes, or Alzheimer's centers. She had experience with this type of work already, and when she wasn't helping strangers wipe their butts, she came home to help her daughter learn how to do it. I learned that as well as how to give a sponge bath while Teresa was sitting on a chair inside of the shower, the same shower that had a hole in the wall that looked into the laundry room, just in the bottom corner, but again, we weren't going to worry about that when Teresa needed so much attention.

I was taught what each pill was that she took. They were organized in her little color-coded pill organizer, and I was taught when to give them to her, to make sure she ate something, and if she got an upset stomach anyway, I was taught how to clean that up.

Teenagers are lacking in some life skills these days, with most not knowing how to boil water, which is incredibly basic but apparently difficult if you've never done it. I was one such teenager. I couldn't cook if my life depended on it. I relied entirely on prepackaged foods, but I could tell you all about Teresa's predicament, and eventually I used my math skills to become a dealer for my family. Or bookkeeper, rather. My mother was the dealer, and I was the bookkeeper. I enjoyed writing and math, and I was good at them. My mother kept a little purse-sized notebook in her top drawer in our bedroom, and I used that to keep track of how many pills Teresa had left of her prescriptions and—this is the best part—how much money was owed to us from family members who had "borrowed" them.

Almost immediately, family hopped on board the Lortab Express. And as I say in my last book, *Raised by Narcotics*, it was easier to tell you who wasn't on that train. Grandma Jane.

Grandma Jane was simply trying to keep us all afloat. She had a small table in the basement, with one single chair and a lamp. The table sat behind the chair that Teresa normally sat in to watch TV and smoke her cigarettes and, well, survive day to day. At that small table set up for only Grandma Jane to use, she kept her checkbook, a pen, a pad of paper, two things of nail polish in beige and burgundy, and her little nail grooming kit.

This is where she would sit and paint her nails and then use her pen, paper, and checkbook to balance our financial lives. This was her office, as much as she could have one.

Along the wall next to the staircase and across from Grandma's little table was a long, old sofa and coffee table where I kept my coloring books and toys. I have a lot of memories of sitting there and playing or coloring while Teresa napped on the couch, before her accident, and after her accident, it became a way to sit with Grandma Jane and sometimes do my nails as well. As long as the adults were not smoking. When they were, I was supposed to go upstairs, but as I grew into a teenager, they forced me out less and less.

We each had a part to play in the family, and we each took turns taking care of Teresa. Grandma worked during the day, and Mom slept because she worked graveyard shifts. While I was out of school for the summer, I took on nursing Teresa and all of her needs until school started back up, and she eventually gained enough strength to do some things on her own. Still it was a struggle, and most of us lost sleep during the first few months after the accident. When she was strong enough to climb back up the stairs for the first time, it was a very similar process to how we had gotten her down there, but that's when we were able to get her into Grandma's car and back over to the hospital for her to learn how to walk again using their rehab pool.

I really loved going, even though I didn't get to go into the pool with her. It was something new and exciting, and I cheered her on while she slowly walked back and forth over the course of about half an hour. Then, either with Grandma Jane or Mom, I would help her get dressed again and back into the car to go home. She only did this about once a week, I believe? And not for that long either. At most, three months. I don't recall how intensive this was, and it was the only type of physical therapy she ended up doing. Very likely due to the fact that we couldn't pay for anything else. Using the pool, pretty much unassisted, was pretty cheap.

And it worked. With the combination of the pool therapy and climbing the stairs to get her there, she gained enough strength to walk on her own again, wipe her own butt, and get her own coffee or pills. Oh, and not just that, she was also able to drive again.

Let's talk about how scary driving is with someone who's constantly high. I feared for my life every single time, but with her ability to drive, I had to rely on her because I wasn't old enough, and Mom was just done doing it for me. Teresa was home, so she might as well, right? It wasn't often, but when she drove me around, she almost always veered out of her lane, shamefully laughed in an almost drunken way, and righted herself.

When you're taking opioids, you should not drive. It is considered a DUI, or driving under the influence. Not many people realize this. When you're taking opioids, or narcotics, for chronic and potentially life-long pain, you just do what you have to and deal with the consequences later. Teresa was at risk of causing harm to not only herself while she was driving, but also her passengers and anyone else on the roads with her. She very nearly put people in her same position by getting behind the wheel again. She was never not on painkillers. Those were now a constant in her life, and no doctors were making any plans to get her off them.

Chapter 10

I Learned It from Watching You, Mom

On my thirteenth birthday, my mother slapped me across the face and called me a "royal b*tch." I apologize for not being able to sensor that one properly. I think that's the hardest thing about this book. My life was uncensored; your life is as well. If I put a little star where the *i* should be, then all is well in the world and your delicate frame of mind is preserved.

I can't tell you what I had done to provoke her, but I was standing in the doorway of my bedroom and minding my own business. She was standing in the hall on the other side. Maybe I had been listening to my music too loudly. Maybe I had back talked the way teenagers are prone to do.

What I can share with you is what my personality was like back then. I was troubled but not the kind of troubled to go out and make friends with the wrong people (that came years later), be part of gangs, or do bad things. Let's throw back to that fifth-grade year when I was bullied because I had refused to take part in the bullying of another. I was not a mean person. I was shy, quiet, reserved, and generally, as they called me in fifth grade, a loner.

Now it was summer again, and my mother was standing in the hallway slapping me and calling me names, for reasons I'm sure were not justifiable.

It was around this time in my life that Mom started losing her mind, not literally (not yet), but as I grew, so did her temper.

Growing up, before we moved in with Grandma Jane and Aunt Teresa, when it was just me, Mom, and Cody in our little house on Center Street in Spanish Fork, Mom had a tendency to hurt Cody. They would scream at each other and break things and try to break each other. Mom had slammed Cody's foot in the door, and before he could remove it from between the wall and the door, she pushed so hard like she was trying to squeeze his foot off of his leg.

She was trying to hurt him. There was the day I came home from school and the coffee table was broken in half. I don't know who broke it. There were the countless times I would hide away in my closet, the great big wardrobe that now reminds me of the book *The Lion, the Witch and the Wardrobe*. I had two on either side of the window in my bedroom, and in the bottom of one was a pile of my stuffed animals, and that's where I would hide while Mom screamed at Cody for any various reason she had justified.

Mom taught me to scream. When I was in trouble or grounded or sent to my room, I would scream at her, "I WANT GRANDMA!!!" Over and over and over again and slam my door repeatedly. That I wasn't hit for this as a child seems to be somewhat of a miracle in my mind. I was spanked, and I was sent to corners to think about what I had done, where usually I just pouted because it was so unfair. Those things honestly seem normal. I didn't get the brunt of what Mom could dish out, not until I was older and Cody was moved out.

Was Mom just doing her best and trying to discipline her children the way she had been disciplined? Had that been her normal?

Now I was thirteen, and Mom had some carryover of those habits, and not only that but she had started taking Teresa's pills too. She was one of the names inside of the little notebook we kept in her top drawer.

At the time, I was blind to what was happening, but after a lot of therapy and looking retrospectively at the past, I can see what was probably happening. Taking drugs like that, recreationally, casually, messes with your brain chemistry. I have some weird memories of Teresa going "crazy" when she wasn't taking her mental health meds, but I have a lot more firsthand experience with my mother losing her grip. Teresa, with both mental health disorders and physical injuries that she was taking medication for, was largely just a druggie. Mellow, slept a lot, barely coherent most of the time, but I also believe part of this was her otherwise gentle personality. I do wonder what Teresa would have been like if she hadn't faced all this adversity that was completely out of her control. Who was she really?

My point is that Mom was in some amount of control of her situation, but how much is entirely up for debate. Was she just a stressed-out single mom with two deadbeat baby daddies who wouldn't have anything to do with their children? And two children she herself didn't know what to do with? Was she just a woman who made mistakes and was trying her best not to feel like they were mistakes? Just a woman full of regret, with her own past and her own pain? Mom also had a past, and it wasn't something I ever really thought about until I was much older. She had an older half brother who terrorized her and, allegedly, sexually molested her. Her parents divorced before that abuse began, and she eventually got pregnant with her first child, Cody, at the age of fifteen.

I don't know how Mom would have described her life if she had taken the time to sit down and write about it, and I hate sitting here and talking about her like she's a villain, but . . .

But, guys, she abused me, and as I mentioned before, I didn't actually see it as abuse until I was thirty years old, sitting in therapy reliving the things she did to me and trying to justify her actions because she was also my friend. At times, she was my best friend. We went to movies together and shared a sense of humor. We laughed a lot, the good belly laughs that I don't seem to know anymore, and we had these hours-long conversations that fulfilled a piece of me that just can't be replicated. There is so much that I miss about my mother, so many wonderful moments that I would do anything to get back, but . . .

But I wouldn't bring her back knowing that she was anything like what I knew of her before. I could never separate those two sides of her. The extreme love and affection with the extreme anger and abuse.

I'm going to share a story now that's not in *Raised by Narcotics*. I wrote it down in a blog post once, but that blog is now long gone, and I don't think anyone felt anything other than pity for me at the situation that happened to me when I was thirteen years old. Blogs and books are different things and serve different purposes. This book is about connecting with you and showing you what you're going through, hopefully well before you turn thirty, and seeing if we can't collectively come up with solutions to create more support for one another because our home lives are so terrible and isolating.

I grew up in Spanish Fork, Utah. Not a town many outside of Utah have heard of, and it's growing now, but when I was a child and teen it was just a backwater town where everyone knew everyone. The most important thing here is not the city I grew up in, but the state. Utah is most well known for the LDS, or Latter-Day Saints, church, aka Mormons. Everyone I knew was Mormon, and my family history is full of Mormon pioneers (on Grandma's side), but Mom considered herself "spiritual" without attending any one organized religion. The brother who molested her went on to serve a mission for the LDS church and rise in the ranks of it as well. I, admittedly, have mixed feelings about this church, but I'm not here to criticize an organization based on my own personal experience or history.

To share a story of my experience is not to sit here and bash the Mormons for what they believe. A statement I wish I had written in my first book, but everyone takes away what they want to hear. I don't have any control over that.

Here's my story:

After I turned thirteen, my mother wanted me to get baptized in the Mormon church. It was not uncommon to have missionaries randomly show up on your doorstep one day and try to share the words of wisdom. This was something we were all fairly used to, and Grandma being a member of the church, albeit not currently active, had what is called "visiting teachers" over a few times a year. Visiting teachers are people who are assigned to you from within the church to come to your home however often they do and talk about the church. My family was still pretty involved with the church even if we didn't go every Sunday, and, of course, having other members of our extended family completely devoted to the church, every wedding and special life event was held in one of said churches. The Mormon church was a huge part of my life, but I didn't consider myself religious. I was only thirteen, however, so what did I know?

Well, I was about to be told. A couple of adorable missionary women showed up at our doorstep, and for whatever reason, Mom had decided it was time for me to be a member. They started coming once a week and sat in our good upstairs living room, out of the way of the cigarette smoke, to talk to me, Grandma Jane, and Mom sitting in silence while I was shown the light.

Eventually, my baptism date was set for October. I had to start attending church and checking off boxes so that I could get baptized.

I was questioning a lot of things in my life at this point. You now have a good chunk of the story and see why I wouldn't necessarily be all smiles and obedience over the task I was given that would dramatically change my life. I needed stability, and this was going to throw me out of my comfort zone again.

Everyone sitting in the room, except for me, could say that they had already been baptized. I think this put more pressure on me and took it off of them to do this thing and become active members again.

Mom outright refused to go to church with me, but I was so scared to go alone. I had already started participating in the young women's activities within the church, and the people just made me nervous. I didn't feel like I fit in, and it was something I struggled with everywhere I went. To have to go sit alone in the masses of families that were nothing like me, that notion was terrifying. I didn't fully understand why I was doing what I was doing, and I didn't feel like the questions I was asking were getting me answers that I felt comfortable with. Nothing about it made any sense to me. Grandma Jane finally volunteered to sit in church with me. She said she would sit in the sacrament meeting, the great big meeting with every member sitting in the same room, and then let me go to my personal classes alone and pick me up after.

I agreed.

We sat in that meeting, and it was testimony day. The day that everyone would share their testimony and why they felt the church was true and talk about their deep love of Christ, our savior. I watched very small children get up and be fed lines by their parents. Whispered in their ears, they were told what to say, and it was all the same. "Hi, my name is . . . and I love Jesus Christ, our savior, and I know the church is true, amen." A few adults came up and said largely the same things, with variations of being able to feel the Holy Spirit.

While I sat listening, and quite frankly bored, I thought to myself, "I don't feel anything, and these adults are just bigger versions of these children who are being told what to feel and what to say."

My Mormon friends and family will not enjoy this part of the book, but I share to show you what I was going through. The internal dialogue inside my head.

I didn't belong, and it was in that moment that I knew. Once it was over, I pulled Grandma Jane into the church hallway and told her, "I can't do this. It doesn't feel right." And she gave me this quietly disappointed look that I remember thinking had a lot more to do with what Mom would think rather than what she thought of me. I wasn't worried about Grandma Jane's judgment. She loved me no matter who I was or what I believed. She drove me home and let me decide for myself what I wanted that day.

My memory gets muddled here. As much as Grandma Jane loved me, she didn't save me from what came next. In fact, I can't remember where she was or what she was doing. If she had left the house to run errands or went downstairs or taken a nap . . . I don't know, but she's gone from this part of my memory.

Mom was furious when I came home. She yelled at me her disappointment and went downstairs and slammed her door.

We no longer shared a room because Cody had married his high school sweetheart and moved out. Mom took his old bedroom and left me to have the one upstairs to myself. I went into my room to change out of my Sunday best and feel generally awful about the entire experience. Now I wouldn't be getting baptized and Mom wouldn't be able to be proud of me, and I hated myself for what I was doing, but I wasn't going to do something that didn't feel right. It wasn't in me to be that person. It never had been. I wouldn't live a lie to make someone else happy.

Teenagers need autonomy, control over their own lives. We are told constantly to be who we want to be, but it's within all these restrictions. Here I had this choice I could make on my own, but it came with consequences. I figured she would scream and yell at me, but I also figured I was kind of used to that already. I would cry, it would hurt, but it would be okay because this wasn't her decision. It was mine.

When I walked out of my room, changed from church and heading toward the bathroom, Mom cornered me in the hallway, screamed in my face, and punched me in the stomach. I was taken by surprise and tried to ball up a fist of my own and hit her back. She was stunned.

Had Cody ever tried to hit back? Could he? Or would he have been taken away because he was a boy? Boys at that time were taught not to hit girls (but they could hit other boys? Or girls could hit girls? The logic there was admittedly lacking during this era), especially not their mothers—it would have looked like he was abusing her. But I could hit back (?), and I did, weakly, and barely made contact with her shoulder because I was so scared but didn't want to cower in the corner of the hallway. I was shaking, and I could see Mom visibly shaking as well. She got this look in her eyes that I can't quite describe, and she ran back downstairs.

Immediately I grabbed the phone off the wall. We didn't each have our own cell phones at that point, still just phones attached to walls. I picked up our cordless phone and held onto it for dear life. I sat on the couch in the living room and sobbed until I had some amount of control and knew whether or not I would be brave enough to make my phone call.

Finally, I dialed Cody's number, and when he picked up, I tried, still sobbing, to tell him that "Mom punched me" and "I can't go to church anymore."

"Alyse! What happened?" he screamed at me through the receiver, worried to death over what had just happened to his little sister. "I'm coming over right now." And he hung up and I sat on the couch until I heard his truck pull into the driveway, still shaking and trying to pull myself together enough to explain properly that I had gone to church, decided I couldn't do it, came home and Mom was mad, and she punched me.

Cody rightfully lost his mind and ran down the stairs to yell at her. I followed behind, sitting on the bottom

of the stairs to listen, and suddenly I heard him screaming, "Alyse! Call 911! She's trying to kill herself!"
I ran into Mom's room where I saw Mom and Cody
struggling over a bottle of pills that Mom was trying to
overdose on. There was a rotary phone in the hallway
right outside of Mom's room, and I used it to dial 911.
Before I could get more than "my mom's trying to kill
herself" out of my mouth, Mom was ripping the phone
out of my hand and slamming the receiver back on the
wall. I ran upstairs to call again on the cordless phone,
but emergency services were already calling me back. I
picked up and told them that Mom was trying to overdose on pills.

An ambulance arrived at our house, and police came
in to check on Mom. They asked her to sit at the kitchen
table while they checked her pupils and monitored her
vitals to see if they needed to rush her to the hospital.
We didn't know if Mom had managed to take any of the
pills or not. While she sat there, I stood at the far end
of the kitchen, watching from the same corner she had
backed me into and punched me in just an hour earlier.
She glared at me with this intensity that still scares me,
even now that she's gone, even now that she's not a
danger to me. The memory still haunts me.

The medics gave her the clear, packed up their things,
and left our house. I never told them or the police offi-
cers that Mom had hurt me. Did she try to overdose

because she had just hit me? Or because I didn't want to go to church? Or because she wanted the attention?

That glare that Mom gave me shut me down into submission. I didn't know what to do or where to go. Cody helped me pack up some things and let me stay with him for a few days, but eventually I went back home. Mom didn't talk to me for weeks. As if the entire thing had been my fault, and this was my punishment. I felt sick inside. I felt guilty for doing that to her. I questioned myself and why I couldn't just believe in all those religious teachings so that she would love me. I started wondering . . .

Should I kill myself?

Chapter II

Today on *Maury*

In the '90s, and even sometimes now, mental health was a joke. A joke we all laughed at on daytime television. *The Maury Povich Show*, *The Jerry Springer Show*, and *The Montel Williams Show* (to name a few) were TV talk shows whose hosts poked fun at basic Americans' lives and used their mental health to get higher ratings for their shows. This is what they lived and breathed on. Here's the big question still being asked today: are they fake?

#RealityTV

As a teenager, and even younger, I watched these shows. I shouldn't have; they weren't meant for me, but when has that ever stopped anyone? Everyone in my generation remembers these people and has their own memories of these shows. Along with everyone else,

I got sucked into these dramatic shows because they showcased a lot of drama. Deadbeat dads, not knowing who the father is, runaway children, makeover or ugly-duckling episodes (where women who were ugly as teens became hot as adults and showed off). Sometimes their secret crushes from high school would be on the show so they could flaunt their stuff and say, "Look at me now!" However fake or real these shows might have been, they took what looked like real-life people and threw their "real-life" problems on public television to show the world how messed up they were.

"At least we're not those people!" Ha ha ha . . . as I sat wondering if maybe my real dad wasn't really my dad, and maybe there was a chance he was someone else who might love me and want to be in my life.

There was one episode I specifically remember, on what I believe was *Maury*, where a young girl, a teenager, wore long sleeve shirts all day, every day to cover up the scars on her arms where she cut herself.

It's hard not to use explicit detail here. I will be intentionally vague because I know that some of you are going through the very same thing and I know that some of you have considered it.

By the time I was fourteen years old, I was so confused about my life and what was happening. That confusion comes from not feeling loved, from living in daily fear of what the people around you think of you, the fear of wondering why your father never loved you and felt justified in leaving you behind, the fear that you'll never accomplish anything or be able to live your dreams. Lost in the numb feeling of being trapped in a situation outside of your control. Not loving yourself because you're too fat and ugly (you are not, but I understand this feeling).

Being a teenager is constantly wondering, fearing, hurting, second-guessing . . .

There will be people who don't understand any of what I've written. I'm glad for that. So, so happy for that. But if you're relating way too hard, just know that you're not alone, and I get it. I so, so get it.

That episode got into my head. I would love to sit and blame it on the fact that I already had a weird fascination with the human body, specifically dead people. I wanted to grow up and become an archaeologist, a woman who traveled the world and dug up ancient cultures and dead people, mummies. I wanted to know how they lived and how they died, and I just wanted nothing more than to be surrounded by the dead. We all have dreams, and this one was mine (and look at me now)!

#ThatsMessedUp

As we grow older, we realize that certain likes and interests fall into certain categories of our culture. I was starting to fall into the "goth" category. Wearing black, listening to heavy metal, enjoying Halloween and horror movies. All things I enjoyed that created a label for me. Let's go ahead and forget that I loved rainbows and puppies and was a Disney princess. My princess days were coming to an end, and this princess was now fascinated with what it might feel like to put a sharp object to her skin and watch herself bleed.

It hurt worse than I imagined, and as I sat in my bedroom, my heavy metal music playing too loudly and black curtains shutting out the sunlight to my room and my soul, I used a piece of glass I picked up off of the floor after pushing over one of my cherished wine glasses that I had started collecting from different places we had traveled to on family road trips, this one from Las Vegas, Nevada.

I didn't want the scars on my arms because I liked summer and enjoyed how my skin looked in the sunshine. Because my grandmother on my father's side was from Mexico, I had a beautiful glow that everyone envied, possibly the only thing anyone envied about me, throughout most of the year. My skin would make any California girl jealous. Instead of cutting up the flesh on my arms, I started slicing up the flesh on the inside of my left ankle. Starting with one little scratch, and it hurt so bad. I only kept going because I wanted so badly to see the blood. I felt desperate. I wanted to be brave enough to do this one thing that no one else would or could do.

It wasn't bravery that drove me to do that. It was emotional devastation of my daily life that drove me to do it. What I quickly realized after the first time I did it was that this physical pain took away my emotional pain, or numbed it, rather. It pushed it aside, and I forgot how broken I felt internally. I don't want to call it joy because nothing about my life was joyful. It was a way of coping with something, having control over something, that left me feeling afraid, confused, lost, and broken.

I will also admit that it was attention. After a time, I would leave my skin broken and bleeding and walk out of my room, blood dripping down my leg. Not enough to cause anything to fall onto the floor but enough to congeal to my skin and leave a nice red line that stopped at the top of my foot. I wondered if anyone would notice that I was bleeding and ask, "Alyse, what happened?" so I could come up with some injury and get their care and attention.

If they ever noticed, they never said anything. If they knew what I was doing, they never talked to me about it. They never asked.

I don't want this entire chapter to be about this, though, and I don't want to put ideas into your head the way that episode did to me. If you're reading this and relating to this, you've already made those decisions. That's the problem. I know now that I wasn't alone in it. I've since seen and heard countless stories of others doing the very same thing, in different ways, but for largely the same reasons. Control. Using a different method of pain to suppress the pain that hurts worse than the physical mutilation of your own body. A different type of addiction.

Why are our emotions harder to handle?

Our mental health matters, and it's still up for debate what these talk shows were doing and the commentary they left on a blood-stained nation. Every problem we face has some level of mental health associated with it. If we could ever treat the two as if they were the same or as if they go hand in hand. One with the other, because they do, but we neglect so much of our emotions and thoughts.

* * *

I don't want to write this book anymore. I get to this point sometimes when I'm writing, and my heart hurts. Are you really living this life right now? The one where you're reading my words and you know exactly how I was feeling? Can I please swoop into your life and be the person for you that my parents never were for me? You matter so much, and you don't see it. You don't feel it. I'm so sorry.

* * *

I wondered what I would write for this chapter, the one where I'm fourteen and confused, hurting, but not entirely sure why. So much of what I see now I did not see when I was in it. I didn't see it when I was fourteen, hurting myself, being a loner in school, and struggling with depression and what was turning into suicidal thoughts.

That's what this chapter is; it's my jumbled-up mess of a life and the scattered thoughts all jumping around from one thing to another.

At this point, I was in junior high school and an introvert. I didn't see myself as an introvert; I saw myself as a loner. The thing they called me in fifth grade, the thing that stuck with me for years after. I became scared of interacting with my peers, always afraid I wouldn't fit in. I wanted to. I tried wearing makeup and tweezing my brows and putting together outfits even if they came from the thrift store or were hand-me-downs from my own mother. I never managed to be on point or, you know, pretty. I struggled a lot with low self-esteem. I was chubby. I wasn't the fattest girl in school, but I also wasn't skinny and beautiful. I never stood a chance at being that person. I ate to comfort myself. I ate to cure boredom. I didn't know what most fruits or vegetables really tasted like. We didn't have those at home. We had cheap cans of SpaghettiOs or ravioli. I craved something my body couldn't find and kept searching for, so I kept eating the only foods we could afford—off-brand processed junk—and never felt satisfied.

Being the loner I was, who was afraid of people and hated looking at herself, or rather as I looked at myself in the mirror, I wondered what I could change to make it better. My mother called me vain because I looked in the mirror so often. I just wanted to be pretty and attractive, and in our society, that means looking in the mirror, fixing your hair just right, and putting on layers of colorful makeup. Anyway, being this person at school, I often found myself in the bathroom in between classes or during lunch. It's how I filled my time and kept to myself. I didn't want to interact, and so I hid. I didn't necessarily see it as hiding until one day as I was standing in the bathroom, hoping to fix myself enough that when I stepped out I would just morph into a different, more beautiful person, altogether, I heard a group of girls talking too loudly and about to come inside. I ran into one of the stalls quickly and sat on the toilet to use the restroom and sat there until they left. I didn't want to interact, and I didn't want to walk out and face the lonely world of wandering the halls alone. For whatever reason, I just couldn't live with myself if I didn't have other people to gravitate toward. People to fit in with. So I hid away in the stalls and waited for them to leave, a new habit I had been forming. They were taking their time and talking. They knew I was in there; it was a smaller bathroom with only three stalls and one was taken.

"She's such a follower," one of the girls said.

"She doesn't have any real friends; she just follows people around. It's so annoying."

"Alyse is such a follower," one said, repeating what the first girl had said, deliberately taunting me as I sat with my pants down on the toilet behind the door. Hiding from the very same people I hadn't wanted to run into in the hallways.

To this day, I don't know exactly who it was that said these things. I have guesses, but that's who I was to everyone at school. A loner. A follower. An annoying quiet girl trying to fit in with nothing to contribute to any group of people she passed in the hallways.

When they finally left, I held in my tears, pulled up my pants, and stood in front of the mirror in the bathroom. I heard the first bell ring, warning students to get to class. Lunch was over. I stood there staring at this person I hated. This girl who was too fat, too shy, too ugly . . . and the tears started running down my face. I couldn't leave the bathroom now and show everyone that I was crying. It would just add to the humiliation of being the person in school who didn't fit in with anyone around her. I waited for the second bell to ring, hoping that when I came out everyone would be in class, teachers and students too preoccupied, their doors closed, to notice me when I pulled open the bathroom door and quickly walked out of the school telling myself that I would just tell my mom I didn't feel good when I got home, go to my room, shut my door, and cry.

Cry and sleep, but instead lay in bed wondering if I had the guts to take the pieces of glass I was hiding in a small jewelry box I had from my childhood and slice it up my arm, the way Mom had described to me once.

Yes. My mother.

Before I had ever started harming myself, my own mother once told me the right way to kill yourself if you were to slit your wrists so you would die faster. Also, the correct way to drown.

Most likely it was a combination of her words and the people on TV that made me wonder if I could do it. That made me start trying, if even only small attempts that didn't count for anything.

* * *

I don't want you to read this anymore. How can such a small child want to hurt or kill themselves? Ignorant adults ask this question all the time. I've since had conversations about this with close friends who then share with me what their childhood was like, and guess what? They were bullied at young ages. They didn't fit in at home. They were lost, lonely, and confused, and yet, we all ask this dumb question: how can this happen?

This is how this happens! And we all hide our pain, physical and emotional. We hide away. Why was the Disney movie *Frozen* so popular? Because Elsa sang what we were all feeling.

F*$#*$&*% Disney!

#LetItGo

sigh

There's hope, right? There must be. I'm still here, aren't I? Still here writing these words and hoping to reach out to you so that you know you're not alone in this world. That I understand your pain even if you feel that no one else around you does. There is at least one person who understands you and what you're dealing with. That person is me. I'm here, okay?!

Chapter 12

There's a Pill for That

Finding peace in a world full of what felt like chaos was nearly impossible. I took to writing, poetry mostly, and no one was surprised that writing is now the thing that keeps me going. I listened to music, as loud as possible, lost myself in it, and wrote angsty poetry. Sad things, beautiful things, angry things . . . this was how I expressed myself. I would sit for hours upon hours in my bedroom with music and a notebook. What I didn't know then was that I was doing myself a huge favor. I had found things that I enjoyed immensely and used them to escape. I was coping.

If I'd had a therapist at this time in my life, they would have recommended to me to do what I was already doing. Writing. I'm not saying that writing is the only way to cope, but it is a much healthier alternative than, say, drugs or cutting yourself. Music as well, even the angry kind, is a healthier way to deal with emotional pain. Thinking that maybe these musicians get it because they wrote words that you understand, so you're not as alone as you feel.

I've also enjoyed creative outlets like painting and drawing. I watch my children now, who create things like jewelry, read books, and play video games (yes, I'm the one mom who says that's okay), and in my adult years, alongside my two kids, we've greatly enjoyed getting outside for long walks anywhere the sidewalks will take us. Our dogs help as well. Animals have a lot of love to give.

I grew up watching my mother love to read. She read constantly while sitting at the kitchen table with a plate of nachos and salsa, her guilty pleasure. I was not as avid a reader as my mom was until *Harry Potter* was released around the time I was thirteen. I did grow up in libraries and old bookstores on Main Street that sold used books. People in these places knew us by name because we came so often. Mom read me stories every night before bed and let me put stickers all over the headboard of my bed if I did a good job reading each day when I was just learning. Reading was a huge outlet for my mother. Getting me to learn to love to read as well was hugely important to her, but the truth was, I didn't love it nearly as much as she did, but again, *Harry Potter* changed all of that.

I believe that J.K. Rowling saved lives with her books. She certainly saved mine. Those books were heaven to me and gave me an appreciation for new worlds outside of the one I was living in, and I guess, in a way, I related to Harry Potter and wished that my own life served some deeper, more magical purpose. I wanted some important wizard to send me a letter inviting me to come live anywhere else and teach me how to appreciate my gifts and use them to become successful.

Being a teenager is difficult, for all the reasons I've already explained. You are so full of hope and wonder, and you know some day you'll grow up and have responsibilities and you also fantasize constantly about exactly how you'll do that. You carry so many ideas for your life and who you'll be, and that's what keeps you going.

That's what kept me going. I had potential. Every teenager has potential. I saw my own even if no one else did. The weird thing about Mom was that she saw it too. I was living in an abusive relationship, with all that it comes with. The hate, the love. The extremes of each. And she loved in extreme ways and had so much pride in the things that I did with my time. She listened to me recite my poetry and applauded me. She hugged me and took pictures of my artwork. She told me I would go on to do amazing things with my life. She had no way of helping me achieve anything, other than to shower me with praise, in between the moments that she was ridiculing me, calling me names, slapping me . . . etc.

I needed her love and praise in a big way. I needed her attention. If she wouldn't see how I was hurting, she would at least see me become successful. I had something to prove to my mother, that I wouldn't become like her.

Maybe Mom gave me just enough good-mothering moments to show me that I was worth something in this life. Just enough to help me scrape by emotionally while I watched her fall apart.

Over the last few years, after the accident and Teresa's new drug addiction to opioids, Mom was finding reasons to get her own drugs. Doctor shopping, as it's called. My entire extended family did this. Everyone was going to doctors to get pills, and the pill swapping within my family only became more complicated because now it wasn't just taking from Teresa; it was taking and borrowing from each other.

The year I was fifteen, Mom would turn forty. The big four-zero. She had been having pain in her arm and hand and had a lump in her throat. During this time, she worked for the Alzheimer's center, where people with Alzheimer's went to live out the remainder of their days. Mom watched a lot of people die. Alzheimer's is the disease of the mind and body that makes you forget who you are and where you are. Mostly in old age, but sometimes in younger people. She cared for these people, dealt with their fiery tempers, and helped them ease their way out of this world. It is a surprising thing for some people to hear about how caring she was. She truly loved these people and had strong connections with many of them. I heard a lot of interesting stories.

This is all to preface a few things that happened this same year:

First, she was diagnosed with cancer, something that was incredibly traumatizing for all of us, which turned out to be untrue after more testing. Then on her fortieth birthday, she was officially diagnosed with lupus, after discovering that the lump in her throat wasn't a tumor but, in fact, an overactive, or underactive (I don't remember which), thyroid. Something that goes hand in hand with lupus, which is an autoimmune disease.

Second, she worked the night shift at the Alzheimer's center alongside a man named Bruce, who drove a motorcycle and thought Mom was cute. He liked her a lot. They flirted a lot, and she had fun stories about him too. He had offered many times to take Mom on his motorcycle, but Mom would always say no. I don't think she felt safe on a vehicle like that.

One day he sexually assaulted her. He took things too far, and Mom came home bawling about it. I don't know exactly what he did, but it was enough for Mom to call the police and have him fired. I heard that he also began making death threats to her, and from this moment onward, she was lost in a world of panic.

Mom celebrated her birthday on October 16, the same day she was diagnosed with lupus. Shortly after, the incident at work occurred.

She already had plenty of doctors prescribing her treatment for pain and inflammation, and now she would also be put on antidepressants, sleeping pills, and muscle relaxers for her new anxiety and panic attacks. She was an insomniac now (she couldn't sleep), who hated her life and was constantly in a fit of shaking and yelling.

There came a day that she didn't get out of bed and didn't go back to work. She could no longer face her life. So much had happened by the time she was forty: being sexually assaulted as a child, being diagnosed with lupus and thyroid issues, being sexually assaulted as a grown woman, being a single mother, and helping to care for her older sister after the car accident.

She stopped reading and started watching a lot of daytime television. Even more than before. She stopped showering and became a shell of the woman we all knew. She let herself become bed ridden. If she had to go somewhere, she would try to put on makeup and get ready, and sometimes that would send her into a complete panic. Then she would yell at anyone within earshot and slam her door shut declaring that it was "just too much!"

This is what my mother became when I was just fifteen years old. She was already hard to deal with before, and now this?!

I had to find ways to handle it. I had to cope. I had no choice. Yes, Mom was going through so much, but by not handling it well herself, she threw on all of us the hardship of living with her and her daily pain and sorrows.

I was scared, and alone, but not alone. I still had Grandma Jane, but I don't think she really knew how to connect with a teenager in my position. We often kept to ourselves. I still had Aunt Teresa, but she was high most of the time or sleeping. I still had Cody, but he worked and had started a new life with his wife. I still had Mandy, but she was dealing with her own broken home miles and miles away from me. I connected with each of them in little ways, but largely, I was on my own.

I learned that year that keeping to myself was the only way to survive. This was the year that I started fantasizing about what it might be like to graduate high school, get a job, and move out. I was finally becoming old enough to gain new kinds of freedom, and I wanted to think about those things to get me through the days. I was smart in school. So smart that I could finish my work really quickly and turn the page over so the jerks next to me wouldn't copy my answers. (They had learned to sit next to me because I had the right answers when they were too lazy to do it themselves, and I was smart enough to sometimes get all of the answers wrong on purpose so that they would fail. I didn't mind failing. I knew the work, and I was making a point. This was my quiet way of standing up for myself.) I knew I had the potential to get out, and that's what I wanted. To grow up and get out. I was also old enough to start taking driver's ed, but that wouldn't be until the end of the school year because my birthday was in the middle of summer.

And I knew that when I turned sixteen, I could get a job, make money, and start taking care of myself without anyone else.

These were the hopes for my future. The things I held onto tightly to keep myself going. To keep waking up in the mornings.

I had heard through the grapevine at school that the local KFC had hired a girl my age, and she was getting paid under the table. Apparently, she had family working there, or they ran the place, I don't know exactly, but it made me hopeful.

My family was always struggling with money, and now that Mom didn't work, the words *homeless* or *living in your car* or *on the streets* were something of a daily threat. I became terrified. My unstable life was becoming unhinged. The threads that held it all together were snapping, and if only I would just turn sixteen, I could make some money! I could save myself.

ALYSE NEIBAUR

I could save us. I could help Grandma, who was struggling to make ends meet on her own, in a family that didn't make sense, and who infuriated her son, my uncle. He came over often to yell at all of us and tell Grandma Jane to "kick them out, they're leaches." We were leaches on Grandma Jane. We ate her resources and had nothing to give back. I wanted to punch him in the face every time he showed up at our door and prove something to everyone! I could and would take care of this family! Why wasn't he helping? Why wasn't anyone helping? What was wrong with my family that no one outside of Grandma Jane would support one another? All they did was take, take, take. Take pills. Take money. Take sanity by screaming at each other. Everyone was at odds. Why?

I called the KFC and asked for a job. They laughed at me and hung up. All I could do now was wait for the day that I would turn sixteen. Living in daily fear that something would be the last straw and it would all come crashing down around us. Around me. Because wherever Mom went, I had to go too. If Mom became homeless, well, I was her responsibility. I was her daughter. I was one of the leaches. I was still a child with no rights. Turning sixteen wouldn't change that. The only thing that would change that was turning eighteen, and that was much further away. Something I almost didn't dare dream of.

Mom was taking an absurd number of pills every day now. She became a different kind of person altogether, and I wasn't sure what was causing it. Was it her illness? Was it the depression? I certainly didn't think it was any of the pills. Those were supposed to help her. That's why doctors gave them to you, right? She wasn't getting better; she was getting worse. She could hardly function as a normal person day to day. She wasn't getting dressed, she wasn't getting out of bed, and she was letting herself rot away in her room, only coming out to get coffee or eat cereal, yell at someone for something, and go back, slamming the door behind her and writing terrible notes for us on her bedroom door so we would leave her alone or, in fact, get her the things she needed and refused to get herself.

Then we switched rooms—I can't remember why—but the change of bedroom was a welcome new commodity for me, mostly because it was in the basement, which made it cooler by default. We didn't have air-conditioning in our house, and summers were miserable. But, as she sleeping in the room right above mine, she began knocking on the floor so that I would run upstairs to see the note she had left on her door. Demanding that I do something for her or she would just keep pounding on the floor until I gave in. I always gave in.

There came a day that I didn't understand. It was in the summer, and I was finally about to turn sixteen. I was taking driver's ed through the school and working on getting my learner's permit. Teresa and Cody were the ones to help me learn how to drive, Cody always being my biggest supporter.

I walked into the kitchen while Grandma and Mom were having a tough conversation. I heard Grandma Jane say this: "You have to make this decision for yourself."

Mom had been having phone conversations with her doctor, and then came the moment that she told Grandma Jane she was ready to go.

Ready to go where? And why did she look so . . . worried and sad? What was happening?

It turned out that Mom was being committed, sent somewhere. To where? A facility in Salt Lake City. For what? I don't know. Drugs, maybe. Mental health, maybe. Both, probably. What I learned is that she had become a danger to herself, and I suddenly had flashbacks to the day she punched me and tried to overdose.

Mom had been diagnosed with not just lupus, but also depression, anxiety, and post-traumatic stress disorder (PTSD). She also had insomnia and restless legs syndrome (that's a real thing). She was also in pain because of her lupus, which she took opioids for, and was puffy from the steroids she took daily for her autoimmune and thyroid issues.

Mom was a mess!

Mom had no friends, no outlet, no job, and now she was going somewhere to be looked after like an infant because she was a danger to herself.

My teenage brain couldn't wrap my head around any of it.

What world was I living in?

Mothers were meant to take care of their children, but mine couldn't function. And she was a danger to herself? How about a danger to me? And yet, I still loved her. I still needed her. I was still scared for her and of losing her.

Anger and confusion were sprouting inside of my heart. I didn't understand the life I lived in anymore. I was being told to be a certain way and do certain things, and yet, I was being sheltered from this huge moment, and no one would tell me what was happening or if I would be allowed to see her or for how long she would be gone.

No one thought to turn around and take this young girl aside, who had very little life experience, and explain to her what was happening to her mother. No one thought that maybe the confusion I was living in was also very terrifying, and I didn't know how to voice it. Maybe they just depended on me staying quiet and keeping to myself. That's a terrible thing to depend on, but I do believe that my family didn't really see me or notice me a lot of the time because of how quiet I always was.

These were some of those moments where I truly needed help but didn't have the know-how to express that. Or the wherewithal to know that I should.

Mom needed some type of support in that moment, and maybe she was trying to get it. I also needed support in that moment, being her only child still at home and being left alone a lot so she could have the space to fall apart. That's considered neglect and is another form of abuse. I was not being given the love, support, or connection I needed to grow into a functional adult. I was often isolated and alone, and to this day, I still struggle with connections to others.

These are lifelong issues you are being handed. Not things you'll grow out of as you age. To make that distinction feels very important here.

Let's move on.

Chapter 13

At Least

You will have moments in your life when you're forced to sit down and count your blessings. It's been proven that being grateful for what you have certainly does do wonders for your mental health. I think this is something we should all practice. I say this, however, to warn you. There's a side to this that most don't see outwardly. The "at least" moments. The moments in which you tell yourself "at least I still have ..." and then use that to suppress what you're dealing with.

At a certain point in life, you need to face the things you're suppressing and stop telling yourself it can always get worse. Yes, it can get worse, and if you keep everything bottled up inside of you, it will get worse. It will not get better. Who got better by keeping to themselves and struggling on their own? No one. No one did that. I won't say it's impossible, but I will say that I don't know a single person who overcame something in life and did so without opening up to someone and getting help.

I know a lot of people who died, though. The ultimate worst-case scenario.

In the case of my mother being sent away to some facility . . . at least my mother was getting help.

I think.

At least I wasn't homeless, yet.

At least I was nearly sixteen and could start looking for a job and then maybe a car.

At least when I didn't have a car of my own, my aunt who was always high could drive me to my new job that was twenty minutes away and try not to kill us.

At least I survived.

At least when I found that new job my family wouldn't start taking advantage of me . . .

Oh, wait.

They did. That's exactly what happened.

At least Cody would take us to visit Mom while she was in the facility.

At least she would try to hug me or kind of pat me on the back once, sit down across the room from me, and stare blankly at the air like a zombie who had lost her soul, and at least I would feel loved.

No, I wouldn't.

At least it would last only a couple of minutes, even if those minutes felt like an eternity, and she wouldn't look back at me as she walked back down the hall to do . . . I don't know what she would do.

At least I would dwell on that moment forever.

At least we would go to the zoo after, where I could look around me at some of my childhood memories, and . . . want to crumble from emotional exhaustion because I missed my mom. I missed my childhood. I missed when she was happy.

At least she used to be happy.

It can always get worse, and if you don't face your problems and talk about them with even just one person, they almost always do get worse.

So much was happening in my life, in our lives as a family, and I had no way of emotionally or mentally navigating through it. I didn't know I was supposed to ask for help, I didn't even fully know that I needed help. I was telling myself "at least" constantly. Some kids were homeless. Some kids were hungry. Some kids were being beaten daily. Some kids were in foster homes, instead of living with their families. Some kids, and I personally knew some of these kids, had it worse than I did. Some kids' parents were in prison. Some kids wouldn't get to see their parents come home for quite a long time, if ever. Some kids might grow up completely without even knowing a nice childhood where they were loved. Some kids were already addicted to the same drugs their parents were taking. Some kids were already in juvie (juvenile hall/court—like prison but for kids). Some kids were already making decisions they didn't understand that would impact the rest of their lives. Some kids would die before they turned eighteen.

At least I wasn't those kids.

As I turned sixteen, my mother would be coming and going from a place that I didn't fully understand. She would be hiding things from me that would take me another fifteen years, my lifetime all over again, to see even a glimpse of. Years after her death.

I got a job at Taco Time, which was too far away (sad because that was also Amanda Jane's first job, and working with her, short as it was, was amazing), and it cost too much gas money to get to and nearly cost me my life because of the way Teresa was driving. I then found a second job working at Wendy's, which was pretty much down the hill from my house and, if I was desperate, I could walk there.

I made a whopping $6.10 per hour. In a single week, I would bring home roughly a hundred dollars (after taxes), which, in my mind and at that age, was A TON of money. I quickly watched it disappear, though. My family needed a lot of help, and when Mom came home from the facilities, she needed prescriptions filled, and someone needed to help with groceries and other things now that she wasn't working. I believe that because she saw me working and helping Grandma Jane provide for our family, she used it to justify her bedridden illness and give up on life.

At least I had a job.

I was sixteen and a junior in high school. One year away from being a senior. I started working part-time and eventually moved to full-time to make more money. The people at Wendy's became my second family. My life became wake up, get ready, go to school, come home, eat a quick snack, go to work. Work until night, come home, go to bed, and do it all over again. I had zero interest in coming home for too long. I still had days off, and I tried to spend them out of the house. I now had not just my job at Wendy's, but also my driver's license. Not surprisingly, I was good at driving. Being raised around cars and trucks with my big brother was now paying off. I started using Mom's car to get around. She wasn't using it.

The tricky part about using her car was asking permission. I now had to be incredibly careful around her, or she would lose her temper and take the car-driving privilege away. That's typical for a teenager to have to deal with. I don't begrudge her that important parenting skill. I begrudge her the fact that she would lose her temper over absolutely nothing and decide one day that I couldn't drive it anymore, just because.

So, in fact, I started leaning on Teresa a bit more. She was happy to lend me her car, if I took care of it, and kept gas in it. I was happy to do so.

Now, at least I had a car, and that car gave me some serious freedom. Driving became a way to escape. Driving became my addiction. To be able to get into the car and just go . . . anywhere . . . wow. That freedom felt like a superpower.

There was one place I always found myself. There was a twisty little road in the middle of nowhere at the base of the mountain where the Spanish Fork River flowed. It was called the River Bottoms. I still find myself driving that same twisty road whenever I visit home, but while I was a teenager and using the cars I had access to, I would use this drive to clear my head. I would drive to a little hill that overlooked the road and the valley. It's quite beautiful. I still sit there sometimes and watch the sunset and reflect on my life and how I ended up where I am now. But as a teenager, those reflective moments were always centered around this one thought: "Should I jump?"

Should I jump from the hill and lose myself and let go of the life I didn't feel that I could handle? I was growing up, my world didn't make sense, and I didn't feel prepared. I didn't feel like I could do it.

While editing my first book, my editor pointed out one of the more powerful statements I made while expressing this moment on the hill: I couldn't allow myself to jump because I was more afraid of not dying on my way down the hill than I was of ending my life. I was so afraid of becoming one of them. What if I survived that attempt but became dependent on them for my survival because I didn't do it right? That thought was scarier to me than ending my life. I couldn't do it because I needed to know that my attempt would work, and too often I didn't trust it.

That is the scariest side of true suicidal contemplation. That is when you know that you mean it. This is terrifying to know about, terrifying to know how that feels, because I know that when it gets as bad as that, that's also when you stop caring if anyone around you knows about it and when you start to think, "What's the way I can die and make it work?"

There's maybe even a little bit of satisfaction in that challenge. People around the world don't understand suicide, but they want it to stop. If they could start by understanding that sentiment, then maybe we could get to a point of making a difference in someone's life BEFORE they get pushed to that thought.

That's some heavy stuff for a book for teens. If you understand that feeling, though, let's get you the help you need. Please.

I don't want you to sit alone in that thought. I want you to grow old like me and go on to change the world because you have the passion and capability to do so.

Chapter 14

The Good Parts

As I take my little microscope and zoom into my teenage years for you, I'm picking out all the bad parts. That's the frustrating thing about life. It is so easy to see the bad and forget all the good. I heard somewhere that it takes ten good memories to offset one bad memory. That means I would have needed more good memories to turn around and see my life as something that wasn't falling apart. As it was, I think I had the opposite. Ten bad memories to one good. But there was good.

I already talked a little about this, but I want to expand on it.

This is so important that I say these things and do it all justice. Do them justice. Mom's legacy shouldn't be that she was an abuser and made mistakes that left me feeling broken. She was that, I hate to say, but not always.

I get envious of people who call their mothers their best friends. Mine was my friend too. She would take me to see movies some Sundays because the theater was less crowded that day of the week. We had the same sense of humor and could laugh over almost anything. Weird music we both liked, shows like *South Park* or *The Simpsons*. Movies I wasn't supposed to watch as I got older . . . etc. We went shopping together, and she would help me pick out makeup and tell me I did a good job after getting all excited to try it out. She helped me pick out outfits to wear when I wasn't feeling confident about myself or my appearance, and she taught me how to stand up for myself because she knew how timid I was.

She was supportive of my dreams and encouraged me to be creative. She listened when I read out loud some of my poetry, and she praised me for a job well done when I drew something pretty or got good grades in school. She saved my important school papers in a scrapbook for me to remind me that I had achieved something already, and really, she wanted the world for me.

We took road trips together to visit my grandfather six hours away, listening to comedians like Jeff Foxworthy and Ellen DeGeneres, and experienced fun things like Disneyland and Las Vegas. She would treat the whole family to ice cream occasionally and always made sure the house was in order and that when the new year of school started, I had new clothes, shoes, and a backpack to take with me. She taught me the value of a dollar, not just with the drugs, but with everything in our household. Groceries, bills, and even how to manage debt. Despite the fact that we had as much debt as we did, and even relied on it to keep moving forward, she showed me that it's important to have good relationships with the people you owe money to and to make payments on time. Never looking a gift horse in the mouth, as the saying goes. Respecting others and their establishments.

And what is probably the most important detail here, she raised me. She took the role of two parents when my father decided to leave before I was born. She did not give up on me, and she did the best she could with what she had. My father ran away. Despite the things that Mom and I went through, at least she was there.

I did it again.

At least.

Yeah, that's a little bit of a silver lining. My father could have given me a beautiful life, it turns out. I wouldn't find out until I was twenty-four, one year before Mom died, that he had, in fact, been married the entire time I was growing up and even had a third child with this woman. Not only did they raise that child together in a loving home, full of stability and normal family things, but he raised her children from her previous marriage.

It is difficult for me not to be angry at him. No child support to me or my mother. No contact. I didn't even know if he existed until a friend of mine accidentally found him on social media. I was already married and had a child of my own. I was leaving that part of my life behind me, and then there he was, with this whole story of being the father I should have had, to someone else, even children who weren't his own.

That infuriates me.

Mom, despite her failings, was there for me.

As was Grandma Jane and Teresa. They were my family. They were the parents I had. I had three imperfect women raising me, doing their best, in a world they didn't understand. We had our good times, and we had our bad times. I don't think Mom or Teresa knew the first thing about raising children, and Grandma Jane had already been there, done that, which is why she was my stability. She understood life in a way none of the rest of us did or possibly could. Grandma Jane instilled a strength within me that I never could have gained from living with only my mother, and Teresa instilled a kindness in me that, again, I couldn't have gotten from my mother alone.

I have wonderful and amazing memories with each of these women. And when one fell short, the other would step in and pick up the pieces.

Maybe that's what family is.

You can only pick up so many pieces, though, before some of your own start falling apart as well.

Chapter 15

Moving Out

Remember how I said Teresa and I celebrated our birthdays together? There were years I hated it and other years when it felt like Christmas. "Oooh, the birthdays are coming! What can I get her?" She would have her German chocolate cake, and I would have my strawberry-frosted Funfetti cake, with my little *Snow White and the Seven Dwarves* set up on top. Tradition!

Turning seventeen was no less the case. I loved holidays in my family because my family was always happy and getting along. Maybe it was all phony baloney, but I needed those moments.

This birthday year, I would be getting my senior pictures taken and looking forward to the last year of high school. I would turn eighteen the summer after. I had done well enough in school, gained enough credits, to kind of coast through it. I was able to work it out so that I only had to go to school the first half of the day and be done by lunch. I had more downtime and was making friends at work. I would even have a boyfriend (gasp) and go to dances . . . blah blah blah . . . I'm getting a little ahead of myself.

That summer, before my senior year started, Teresa also had her own opportunity. She was maybe the healthiest she had ever been, which honestly isn't saying all that much, but mentally speaking, she was doing a good job keeping herself together. Mom was falling apart, but this wasn't about Mom.

Every so often, Teresa would try to live on her own and see how it worked out. Mostly, this was before I moved in with them. This would be the first time she would try it since that day that Mom and I moved in.

Grandpa Bill lived in sunny St. George, Utah. The southern part of Utah, two hours outside of Las Vegas. The place I spent nearly every summer of my teen years, road-tripping down with Mom, Teresa, and sometimes Amanda Jane. We were always happy there with him.

He took good care of his daughters. He made sure they had reliable cars to get them—and inadvertently, his granddaughter—where they needed to go and made sure they were never wanting in any way. Honestly his intervention is probably what saved us countless times from actually becoming homeless. He kept himself at a good distance from the drama but stepped in when necessary. He was genuinely a good man. I loved him dearly. Everyone did.

The year that I turned seventeen and Teresa turned forty-three (2003), Grandpa Bill would help Teresa rent a small studio apartment in St. George close to his home. That summer, right after our birthdays, we would help her pack up a few of her things and move down.

It was rather exciting, in so many ways. For her and for the rest of us. She had a lot of her friends down there—somehow they had all migrated down south. I couldn't tell you why, but that's where her life was now. Moving down made sense, and she would be close to Grandpa, who would make sure she was okay.

What surprised me were my own mother-hen-like worries.

Do you have younger siblings? If you do, I'm sure you'll understand this part.

Teresa had taken care of me for years when I was young and Mom was working, then roles changed after her accident and I started taking care of her. Suddenly I was worried she wouldn't take her pills at the right times or with the right food or remember to eat altogether and get sick. Who was going to make her coffee? Who was going to be sorting her pills for her? Who was going to remember if she forgot anything? Who was going to keep her from killing herself, basically? There were some tricky logistics to her situation, with mental health and the narcotics she took daily for the pain she

ALYSE NEIBAUR

still lived with from her broken back in that accident that was now about six years behind us.

She was also taking her food stamps with her. Something the rest of us would have to learn to live without. Between Grandma Jane and I, though, we were making it.

It was quite a celebration to take her down, set her up, and get to walk through her tiny studio. It had a big glass door that opened right up to the orange desert that I had grown up loving so much, and occasionally you could see lizards scampering about. It faced the direction of the sunrise, and I could only imagine waking up to that beautiful sunshine every day.

The whole situation felt temporary. I assumed she would be back. It was just a short almost vacation, but for her, and I think everyone else, this was a big deal. A huge deal. Teresa was moving out on her own. Permanently.

Teresa, out on her own again, forging her own way at the tender age of forty-three, and I did not take it seriously, but I think that was subconscious. Something I was unaware of within myself. To have a little anxiety watching her leave the nest, to miss her, a little teeny tiny bit . . . I don't think that's something I would have admitted out loud back then.

What really happened to me was envy. I was crazy jealous. And I needed to know how to do this on my own in just one short year. One more year, and this could be me. Me moving out. Maybe if Mom and Grandma could handle watching Teresa go, then they could let me go too. It made more sense. I had more potential than my drug-addicted, bipolar aunt. Ouch, I feel terrible that I just said that.

For now, we would be happy for her. And we would stay in St. George for a week or so, soak up the sunshine, watch my skin turn brown, and come home feeling rejuvenated.

But when we got home, it was just me and Mom and Grandma Jane.

There was a piece missing. Teresa. She was our peace.

That's poetic, isn't it? Our missing . . . peace. She calmed us all, in her strange way.

We could still call her. We could still go visit, but now she was doing her own thing, and we couldn't really worry about it.

Except that it was just as I had subconsciously predicted. Short lived. It lasted maybe three months, and I believe I'm being generous.

Grandpa Bill lost his mind. She was driving him crazy, and all my worries pretty much came true. She stopped taking the important meds, the ones for her mental health. After the first time that happened, it was really all downhill from there. She was getting high and drunk with her longtime girlfriend and her deadbeat friends. Falling into the wrong crowds, if you can at such an age. They used her, manipulated her, took from her. She ran out of pills, and she ran out of sanity. She had to come back. Quickly.

She was a mess when she came back. Out of all the memories I have of her being off her meds or drunk or high, this was the worst moment I had ever experienced with her.

She tried to kill my mother.

Straight-up murder.

Knife-to-the-bedsheets-as-my-mother-slept murder.

But my mother hadn't been in her bed. That was the only thing that saved her life. Where had she been? It hadn't been the middle of the night. It was maybe evening, at best, and my mother walked in on Teresa stabbing her bed and trying to kill the person she thought should have been there.

Lots of yelling, screaming, profanities.

I had never heard Teresa yell, until that moment, and I can't tell you what she yelled because she was incoherent. It was gibberish. Teresa came back a scary kind of person, and it took a while to get her back to normal.

Mom's solution: drug her up. Get her back on her normal pills and get her high enough to fall asleep.

It pretty much worked.

I explain this situation because there's quite a bit in here that I missed completely, and only in retrospect can I even slightly open my eyes to the reality of what might have happened.

Teresa did, in fact, try to stab my mother in her bed. That's completely true. Everything I wrote, totally true. It's the missing moments . . .

When we took Teresa down to St. George, and I spent my days at the pool like always or watched TV at Grandpa's house or walked on the trail behind his house looking for lizards and coyotes . . .

Where was Mom?

When Mom went to visit Teresa, did she . . . did she do the same things? Was she also getting high and wasted on who knows what?

Did Mom deliberately sabotage Teresa's chance at being independent so that she would come back home, so that she could continue manipulating her to get the drugs she was so used to taking from her?

These aren't questions I started asking until years after they were all dead.

Why did Teresa go crazy and try to kill Mom?

I may never know. Like I said, they're all dead.

But how did they die?

Such fun questions. My life feels like a murder mystery now. I do believe they were killed, but not in the traditional, scary horror movie kind of way.

I was seventeen. Teresa was forty-three. It took some time to get her back to normal, but we got there, and by Halloween, well, it was as normal as it ever gets.

Here is what I did know: Teresa was building a tolerance to the drugs she was taking. This may have contributed to how she handled living on her own. After taking such heavy opioids for so many years, eventually her body got used to it and needed higher or stronger doses to continue fighting off the pain. She was prescribed different varieties from Lortab to Percocet to OxyContin to what would, in this particular year, become the fentanyl patch. Not a pill. A pain patch that was adhered to the skin and through the tiny pores on her body the medicine would slowly release over time. It was stronger than anything she had taken before and worked all day long. Wonderful!

Mom was a broken person. She was convinced that she would die of lupus, and in my spare time, I found myself on a computer at either the high school or the library researching her illness. I would pay ten cents per page to have them print off my findings and bring them home to discuss with Mom. Poor choice on my part, hoping to find a way for her to find her own silver linings and cope with her illness. In fact, I think I did the opposite and fueled her deathbed fire. She was going to believe what she wanted to believe, and lupus would eventually kill her, or so she kept telling herself and me: "Alyse, I don't know how much longer I have left . . ."

So? What, Mom? You want me to sell all your belongings for whatever I can get and run away and start my own life? Because you never considered that maybe you should start a savings account for either of your children? Or maybe they would want to go to college? Or . . .

"Sure, Mom, I'll go get you more ice cream. Teresa, do you want anything?"

Grandma Jane, bless her heart, was depressed. Truest case of depression I have ever witnessed. She was keeping to herself more and more. Her funny stories about work long gone. She had tried to retire from her many dedicated years at the explosives factory. Her only trophy was a cute little clock that looked like it was attached to dynamite, about to count down to a big explosion. Her retirement fund ran out quickly, she took a second mortgage on the house, and started working for Walmart as a door greeter. She quickly realized that not only was the position well beneath her, but so was the company. She walked out, refusing to go back. We all listened to her rave about it for an afternoon, and she went back to bed.

She slept every afternoon. Woke up, had her coffee, worked in her garden in the warm weather, and took a lot of naps in the winter. She stayed away from the drama. Away from the rest of us. Eventually she picked up another job at a bookbinding factory downtown, but this life was becoming too much for her.

I had my schoolwork and my job and even my friends at work. I met a cute boy at my job, and it turned out he was a junior at the same high school. We started dating as much as you can date a Mormon boy—his mom had rules about dating. He could only take me out every fifth date he had, and he wasn't making efforts to go on those other dates. Truth is, she didn't like me. I wasn't Mormon. Maybe they had that rule as a family, but she also hated me. I tried going to church with him a couple of times, holding his hand while people gave their testimonies. I did it for him because I was so enamored with him. He took me to one dance. I spent money I was hiding away to buy a dress from a seamstress down the street. She helped me tailor the dress a little bit and added the flowy sleeves I really liked. I missed prom later in the year because of it.

I'm not entirely sure he considered me his girlfriend, but things went on like that until the following spring.

He, along with two other coworkers of ours, were my best friends. The three of them were my world. To this day, I cherish each of those relationships, although I don't think they know it. We all eventually went our separate ways, but they gave me a lot to hold onto in a time of my life that was truly painful for me.

My Wendy's crew was my second family. Even my bosses. It was at this point in my life that I was finally able to start opening up about what was going on at home. Not fully, just little bits and pieces, and the longer I worked there, the more they got to know cute, shy, quiet Alyse. The more they got to know me, the more they saw my emotions right on my sleeves, and so they asked. They asked how I was doing, what was going on.

In those moments, I had people to confide in. I had people to tell that I was struggling emotionally, financially . . . etc. As employees, we got a huge discount, but often they would let me walk out at the end of my shift with leftovers, forgotten orders, or orders that people brought back in because things were made incorrectly. Things to tide me over so that I didn't have to burden my family by eating our groceries at home. Food that was for them anyway. Mostly it was just ice cream and cereal.

At the end of this chapter, I just feel tired. That didn't really go anywhere, did it? I explained some things and kind of rambled until we ended up here. There's a good metaphor for life. The thing we call autopilot. You just go with the flow, and before you know it, time has passed. Maybe this helps to explain the disconnection I was feeling toward my family. We were all just trying to survive. One stupid day at a time. Each day was its own, and during none of our days were we thinking about where we would end up next. At this point, it just was what it was.

Maybe I was coasting a little more freely because I had people to lean on. People who cared about me— wasn't that a novel experience. We must move forward, however, even if I don't know how to end this chapter.

Chapter 16

The Day She Died

I considered copying and pasting what I wrote in the last book, but some information is just too traumatizing. I have messages to get across without handing you visual trauma. Now I'm struggling how to tell you how Teresa died.

It's not a secret, hasn't been a secret, and I bet, after all you just read, that you can guess where this is going.

She overdosed.

On painkillers, opioids.

On accident.

Maybe.

I'll tell you how we got there. I was still seventeen, and she was forty-three. She died on the afternoon of March 10, 2004, but I was the one who found her two days earlier. It's complicated. She was making weird noises in her sleep, but I thought it was snoring so I went back to bed (hint: this is what an overdose looks and sounds like). I didn't realize it was an overdose. I had no experience in understanding what that might look like, and naloxone was not an option back then. Likely, we wouldn't have had it on hand even if it had been. Many families still don't. With the severity of what she was going through, it wouldn't have helped anyway. Naloxone can save a life within minutes of an overdose, but she was far beyond that.

What is a single life worth?

Another book for another day, or how about this: I'll tell you when you're older.

Our world is built on marketing campaigns. Naloxone is no different. It's giving some of us an excuse to use. What my family needed was not an excuse to continue using, but a means of actual support to get off of the drugs that were messing with their brain chemistry or some kind of family support to hold us together in these difficult times so we could be a little more patient with one another because, for at least one of us, these heavy narcotics were necessary to battle the daily pain.

Naloxone should be mandatory alongside any prescription opioid, or narcotic. It should also be thoroughly explained to each member in the household, as well as given with a list of side effects and overdose symptoms to look for.

Let's continue . . .

I'm lucky that on the night before I would wake up and find her unresponsive, she and I had a positive interaction over a CD I had just purchased. Music. Something we both enjoyed. She gave me a hug and a kiss on the cheek, and we said goodnight with smiles on our faces.

What I didn't know, what she didn't tell anyone, was that she was in more pain than normal, and all she wanted to do was sleep.

The prescription she had at that time was the fentanyl patch, fairly new to her and later taken off the market for causing—you guessed it—death. We were called by the pharmacy two weeks after she died. Mom had fun with that one because sometimes you need to be able to laugh. It's a messed-up, sick joke, but the joke was on us, really.

Teresa had put one on throughout the day.

To take the pain away.

(That's a fun little rhyme.)

The pain she had been living with for six, nearly seven, years of her life. Pain that would haunt her for the rest of her life, however long that might have been.

Before she went to bed, she put on a second patch.

As she slept, she had a stroke, caused by the second patch.

Whether or not she knew what she was doing is not something any of the rest of us are aware of. She certainly had a stack of reasons to consider suicide. We all kind of did. I wouldn't blame her if that had been her choice. I'm afraid, though, that it wasn't. All the signs pointed toward accidental overdose. It was a new medication, one that would hopefully help more than the others that she had built a tolerance to. And, of course, she wasn't the only one to die this way or to get the phone call a few weeks later that putting on just one patch could end your life.

We later found, written in a journal in the little gray filing cabinet she used as a dresser, with very few words written inside of it, these words: "I just don't want to be in pain anymore." Not signed. Not dated. Somewhere in the middle of the little book. No indication that it had been written as a suicide note, just a little aside from Aunt Teresa that it sucked being in that kind of pain. Just a few words that she knew what it did to our family. That it hurt her more than it hurt any of the rest of us.

I'm sorry, Teresa, for your pain. Truly. Deeply. Sorry.

Mom was the person to recognize what Teresa was going through; she had seen it many times before in the patients she took care of at the Alzheimer's home. The snoring noise that Teresa had made was something Mom called the "death rattle."

Mom handled it poorly because she handled every-thing poorly. I didn't know that Teresa was dying. I didn't know what was happening; I just knew she was breathing funny and wouldn't wake up. Mom was hysterical and splashing water in her face. She forced me out of the room and yelled at me. Typical.

Eventually emergency services were called, and after trying to resuscitate Teresa and failing, they rushed her to the hospital where she was declared brain dead.

After that, it was just a waiting game to tell family, talk to doctors, and pull the plug on a life we had already lost.

It was March 10, 2004, and Teresa was gone.

There is no way to understand how the loss of a life close to you will affect you until it happens. She and I had butted heads so many times over the years that I had found myself wishing for her to die countless times. I just wanted a better life. She wanted a better life. We all wanted a better life.

If that's what we all wanted, then why was it ending like this?

She was the first to die.

Four years later, it would be Grandma Jane's turn on June 15, 2008.

Four years after that, it would be Mom's turn on January 24, 2012.

I called this the four-year curse. And I was terrified when the new year rolled over into 2016. It's okay; it finally stopped. The year 2020 still scares me irrationally, but that's what trauma does to you.

They didn't all die of overdoses, but they did all die from having strokes. Teresa's death was the only one considered an overdose, although I have my suspicions that Mom's death should have been considered one as well because she died in pretty much the same fashion, except that she was homeless and alone. Likely shooting up heroin or some other variety of street drugs, maybe laced with fentanyl because that's trendy these days.

Grandma died of old-person problems. Her stroke likely happened because she was a heavy smoker for most of her life, but she lived to be seventy-two years old. That's pretty good. Her quality of life was absolute garbage, but she made it to old age.

In the end, I was left with just my mother. A terrifying reality.

Let's get back to Teresa though.

I was a senior in high school. Doing surprisingly well for myself. Sort of coasting through it, keeping my job and myself all together. But when she died, I lost myself. I kept coasting. I didn't think I was allowed to be sad. She was just an aunt, after all. She wasn't my parent. She wasn't my sibling. Just Aunt Teresa, with whom I had shared a home for half of my life. The person who helped raise me when I was little because Mom had to work a lot. The person who gave me chocolate milk, played Barbies with me, colored with me, took me out for ice cream, bought me toys when she had money, and generally spoiled me as if I had been her own. The person I shared a birthday with. The person I nursed and rooted for when she broke her back. The person

I worried about when she was left alone, like a small child incapable of caring for themselves.

I was devastated.

Someone took my comfort zone and killed it.

Did opioids kill her? Did she kill herself? Were doctors to blame for this? Big Pharma? The family who created opioids as we know them today?

I had to keep moving forward, but I didn't know what to do with this new pain. A pain I didn't recognize or understand. A pain that would grow and grow over the next eight years until I didn't recognize myself anymore. A pain I would carry into adulthood and inflict upon my own children, my soon-to-be-teenaged daughter.

I never got help for that pain. Or at least, I mean, I think I tried to once, but they just gave me pills for it.

Chapter 17

Destruction

Yes, I eventually sought help after I turned thirty. That's thirteen years after the first death, though. What happened in those thirteen years? That's what *Raised by Narcotics* is all about. That's the one your parents should read. My life was a mess! Beautiful on the outside—in fact, you could at me and think, "Oh, she has everything!" But on the inside, I wanted to tear myself apart, and despite having children of my own, a new little family of my own, those suicidal thoughts never went away. They only got worse.

I don't want you to turn into that. That's why I'm writing this second book. A book I don't want you to read at all, but because of what you're going through, you need to. You need to see that you deserve support and love and enough compassion to help you so that when you're looking at thirty, you're not like me wondering if it was all worth it. I deserved much better too, and I see that now. I see that if I had taken my own action to get the support I definitely needed, maybe everything in my life could have been handled differently.

When I was seventeen, the spring before my eighteenth birthday, the one where I become an adult, the first one without my birthday buddy, I was self-destructing.

I started having panic attacks at work. I didn't know that was what was happening. Work was sometimes stressful. Working in fast food is. People are demanding, and everyone wants everything done quickly. Sometimes we were short staffed, but that didn't mean we didn't still have lunch or dinner rushes to get through. What I used to be able to handle, and even thrive on, I started losing control over. I started losing my ability to breathe through the chaos. I was irritable and would easily lose my temper and then fall apart crying because everything felt like it was caving in on me. My boss was incredibly understanding. If it got bad enough that I started hyperventilating and crying, she would let me go into her office, close the door, and cry. Be alone, away from the madness, and lose myself in all the emotions I had bottled up for the last six-plus years of my life. She ended up putting me on drive-through duty, something less intense, so I could try to cope with my struggle to breathe and still be an active member of our crew, who needed me. I couldn't just abandon them, and I still needed the money, plus I was incredibly embarrassed by it. I couldn't be like Mom and let this thing pull me down with it and lose control. I needed to fight to stay alive. At least that's how it felt.

Losing Teresa was my breaking point. It was my last straw.

Guess who was mad at me for it? Yep, Mom. Because no one on earth would ever understand what Mom was going through. Mom had lost *her* best friend! The only person in the world who understood *her*! The only person *she* could talk to! Teresa was everything to *her*, and now she was gone, and what the heck (Mom didn't say heck) was wrong with *me*?! She wasn't my sister; she wasn't my best friend . . . I had no idea what *Mom* was going through!

All her words to me.

Serious eye roll. Mom was very melodramatic. And I do believe that because she believed it so hard, that her emotional struggle was very real for her. She was right; I didn't understand her. But I did have my own pain and to be told it was stupid? I had not-nice words for my mother going through my head, and I stopped caring what she was going through.

Not before my one last attempt to get her to care about me though. I asked her to go see a doctor with me because I was a mess and I didn't understand what was happening to me. I felt like I should have been able to control it, but I couldn't, and with all the talk around my house for years about depression and anxiety . . . I wondered if I had any of that. It kind of made sense to me. The struggle to breathe when I was in high-stress situations. That feeling that something was sitting in my chest blocking my air from getting into my lungs. Random stomach pains. The overwhelming urge to both cry and fall over and never get back up. It felt sleepy, like exhaustion. My body felt heavy like I couldn't carry it anymore, and I needed to be flat on the ground. It's a weird feeling. I later developed a cold, shaky feeling as well, like I was shivering all over, or mostly in my legs and arms. My muscles would tense up, quiver, and release. This last one still happens, especially when I'm writing about my experiences or talking about them with someone.

I say all of this now with information. Information I want to give you.

I cannot stress this enough. I did not know any of that, any of the signs and symptoms of depression or anxiety. I did not know that I needed to talk to someone. I did not know what was happening to me. My clarity came after I turned thirty and finally saw a therapist and she had to witness my complete, whole-body chaos.

I asked Mom to go to the doctor with me when I was seventeen. She did, but she gave me a hard time for it the entire visit because she had all the stress and couldn't believe I was asking her to go through it all so that I could see someone about my not-real, made-up, teenaged angst.

My appointment was very short.

I sat down with the doctor, who asked me, "What's going on?"

Where I then explained, very timidly, very ashamed of myself and all I was feeling, that I still cut myself and "I think I have depression."

He asked me to show him where I cut myself, and I did. What I had realized before going to the doctor, one of the things that prompted me to go, actually, was that despite the physical pain I was creating for myself, in absolute desperation at this point, it was making my overall emotional pain worse, not better. Nothing was taking away how I was feeling, not even this one little escape that I had. It sounds silly to say that out loud, but it made me feel even more out of control. Even more lost and hopeless.

And saying that to this man who didn't seem to care about me in the least, that I thought I might have depression while this woman, my mother, hovered over me with her "Sorry, Doctor. Teenagers and their drama, am I right?" stare, I felt so vulnerable and scared of what he must think of me. This teenager he didn't know, who had lost her will to live for very valid reasons, but a mother who was impatiently taking care of her daughter out of the kindness of her heart because what is motherhood if not unconditional love and sacrifice?

He didn't know her.

He didn't know me.

He didn't know our situation, and I was too scared to talk about it, especially in front of her. Only God knew what awaited me at home if I said something she didn't appreciate strangers being told about us.

So, as ever, I was handed my very first prescription for my very own made-up depression.

My pills were called Cymbalta. As the doctor put it, "a mild antidepressant."

Mild.

Because what I was dealing with was a mild case of teenage angst.

Well, shoot.

That was my one attempt at seeking help, and the entire experience nearly ate me alive. I took those pills every day for two years. I relied on them. I needed them to survive. They did absolutely nothing for my anxiety, but they helped me feel a little more numb to my overall emotions. I stopped cutting myself for a little while and made a goal to try to put that behind me. I was about to officially become an adult. I had my own drugs to take now, just like everyone else, and it was time to take control of my life with what very little life had to offer me.

Chapter 18

Let's Have a Chat

Let's talk about turning eighteen in this country, the beautiful United States of America, and all that it represents.

The birthday card my big brother, Cody, gave me on my first solo birthday pretty much nailed it: "Now you're old enough to go to prison!"

Yaaaaayyyyyy . . .

Can I add emojis yet? Has that become an option while I've been writing?

Get me some Napoleon Dynamite "yeeeeeessssss" GIF action going, someone?! Anyone?

Yes. Now I was an adult. If I messed up real good, I could get myself put in a cell and forgotten. Woo!

I didn't do that, but I really feel like the image there is good for everyone to hold onto. When you turn eighteen, your life is now yours.

Mostly, sort of, kind of. Mmmhmm.

All I remember of that day is that card and standing in a photograph with my mom and Grandma Jane. Good old birthdays, gotta love 'em. Brings everyone together. I was a little dead inside because my birthday buddy was actually dead. Despite my efforts to graduate high school, I had found myself scared to death that I wouldn't. If I did, I would barely scrape through by the skin of my teeth. Even while walking at the graduation ceremony, I didn't know yet if I would be handed a real diploma or if I would be told I needed a few extra credits. That was a weird moment in my life. Celebrating and crossing my fingers that it meant something. At least the photo evidence of the day would stick around until I did.

After Teresa died and I fell apart, coasting through school became actual coasting. My teachers were nice enough to allow me to leave class if I felt that I couldn't emotionally handle being in class. So I left a lot. I was told to sit in the counselor's office, and I did. She attempted to talk to me all of twice, maybe, about my emotional issues, but her biggest job was trying to get me to sort out my dreams, of which I only had one, and I would never be able to afford it anyway, so what was the point? She tried to talk to me about college and, if I was really interested in what I wanted to be when I grew up, where I might try to go. My interest was archaeology, very specific, and not offered anywhere near me at that time. At least not anywhere I could go. It was offered at Brigham Young University in Provo, Utah, but you had to attend their church to go there (Mormons). I did not want to try to attempt that. She gave me a brochure for it regardless.

That's how my school counselor helped me achieve my dreams.

#Not

So my dreams were dead. I knew it the day we buried Teresa six feet in the ground. I was suddenly not looking forward to becoming an adult. Turns out I did graduate, despite nearly giving up on my life entirely. My teachers had mercy on my lost soul and gave me passing grades so that my walk with my cap and gown had meant something.

You know, in looking back on that, at least there were some people who cared about my welfare, if even only to do that one little thing for me. To give me a chance to say I graduated high school because if I hadn't, who knows if I would have had the state of mind to finish a few measly credits. My biggest dreams were to go to college and become something amazing and take care of myself. Even though I would never have those dreams become a reality, to have that piece of paper to take with me into job interviews in the coming years made a world of difference in my life.

Thank you, teachers at Spanish Fork High School.

Thank you, teachers everywhere. If I could go to college now, I would want to be a teacher when I grow up. You're all the true heroes here. At least in my book.

wink

I managed to graduate and go on to have a slow and meaningless summer at my job at Wendy's that I couldn't handle. I had my big eighteenth birthday, don't remember it, and went on to feel sorry for myself as I watched my best friends go off and make plans with their lives. Go to college. Have futures. Futures I would never have.

I felt really, really sorry for myself. It was very painful to be around them while they talked about college and careers. I ended up breaking up with my at-the-time high school sweetheart. He didn't understand me. I didn't understand him either. I didn't understand his family and the weird church values. I was over it. I wrote him a letter, he was understanding, and we went on being distant friends until that whole thing just faded entirely away. It wasn't a huge deal. In fact, I think he was relieved. Have we talked about identity issues yet? I think he was dating me to cover up that he liked boys. I'm just happy for him that he's living a more genuine life now and that he gave me the friendship that he did when I needed it most. There was a short time where

I was angry about it because I felt used, but aren't we all struggling? He was afraid of something, and I was afraid of something different. We leaned on each other in weird ways and gave each other something no one else could at that time in our lives. So thank you, high school sweetheart. You are still super important to me.

I didn't know what I was going to do with my life, and I couldn't afford to go anywhere. Not even community college. Not even a trade school. Nothing.

This was where my life got complicated. I knew I needed to do something, or I would just end up like Mom and Teresa, either dead or waiting to die while I increased the number of drugs I was taking over the course of my life.

That was a very real possibility for me. Maybe my only real opportunity. That was terrifying. That was my easy answer. That was my default. I was already on that path.

Mom started looking at the army for me. The army. Guys. The army. Can you imagine this broken shell of a girl in the army? I can't even.

#GIJane

The only thing that kept me out of that was being too fat to get in. I weighed 192 pounds. I needed to lose weight but didn't know the first thing about diet and exercise. For the first time in my life, my fatness came in handy.

That option was out. Although, of course, it left me looking at myself in the mirror and feeling worthless and, quite honestly, very alone.

My last resort: Job Corps.

I am still considering writing a book about this experience.

I went. I hated it. It changed my life in weird ways, and I came back home with almost nothing to show for it, unless you count the weird life experience I gained that helped me write my first book years and years later.

It was six months of the first year of my adulthood wasted. Unless I can turn it into something positive for someone else, which seems to be what my life is all about.

From September 2004 to March 2005, I found myself inside of a facility that could otherwise be mistaken for—you guessed it—prison.

Cody had been right.

The types of people who go to Job Corps are as follows: incredibly poor people and criminals being given a second chance in a different type of facility that isn't actually prison.

Was Mom laughing at me behind my back while I was there? Who knows? She seemed supportive-ish. I honestly can't quite tell as I look back on my memories here. She wanted me out, and when I called bawling after the first few nights there, she was as irate as ever and hung up the phone on me!

This happened after it became clear to me that I was just a "piece of meat" as it was said around prison—I mean campus—and that it would be hard to hold onto my belongings because they were being stolen already, including my favorite pair of jeans, and, dude, I already didn't have a lot. Okay! I was poor. Really, really poor. And the things I did have to bring with me were being swiped.

Where was I? What on earth was this life I was living? All in the name of education? What education? This place where I had to sign a piece of paper promising not to eat the paint on the walls in an attempt to get high . . .

Good God! Really?

That was a weird experience, and like I said, because it's what I do, I'll write a book about it someday because it gets even weirder than that.

One full year after Teresa had passed away, I came home from that nonsense. I tried to hide it behind the things I had also left behind. My job. My friends. My . . . life.

I got my job back. Most of my friends were gone off to college. I came back to new coworkers; some faces I recognized because they were younger and attending the same high school that was now solidly a year in my past. A comfort zone that had changed. Coming full circle and swinging back into emotions I had carried with me from that fifth-grade year of my life.

Everything had changed, and I didn't recognize myself anymore.

sigh

Now what?

Chapter 19

Impossible

Graduating high school is a big deal, and when you're in the middle of mapping out the rest of your life in the years that will follow your graduation, you will discover that there are many options. Hopefully, unlike myself, you'll have guidance to resources like scholarships and financial aid or be taught the value of saving your money to afford the things in life that will make a difference in your future. Like your education.

Amanda Jane didn't spend time being a victim to her situation. She shoved everyone aside and took care of herself. She got herself into beauty school, and all the time I was in the Job Corps, she was trying to convince me that I should have stayed and gone to school with her. Amanda, I agree completely. I wish I could go back to this moment and do the same, but life was so much different for both of us.

She had her own struggles with health, and family, and obviously suffered the same loss when Teresa died. We all did. Somehow, though, she harnessed the strength that Grandma Jane had tried to instill in us and pushed forward into the only path that made sense for her. And Amanda Jane yelled at me when I insisted on being the broken girl I was turning into. She was sad to see it happen, and in the few moments we had alone together, sitting in her little car that had cost her $600, eating ninety-nine-cent cheeseburgers and french fries, she shared her honesty with me and that she didn't like who I was becoming.

Job Corps had changed me. Within those walls, I had started trying drugs, hanging out with the wrong people, and coming home depressed and stubbornly holding onto a dream that was never going to be my reality. I didn't want to go to hair school with her, but I did want to be with her, and I didn't have other options. I didn't even have that as an option, really.

One person, alone, cannot make it in this world unless they have one of two things: money or credit. If you have enough money, you can have pretty much anything you want. I didn't. If you have credit, you can get a loan to go to school, buy a car, buy a house. I didn't have that either. The next thing would be a cosigner, someone with good credit who could help you secure a loan to get ahead, basically assuring the bank that you will pay it back—or they will.

Usually this person is your parent or guardian. Who else on this planet would do something like that for you? When school can cost tens of thousands of dollars, and you decide "hey, I can't pay this anymore" or make a bad decision and stop paying, the responsibility lands on this other person, and that's a big deal! That can mess up their financial future, their credit score, and their life. Your decisions could potentially screw up someone else's life, but you also cannot do it alone.

To get started, you always need to have money or know someone with money. One way to get money is with debt. Debt is also how you build your credit score, and when you turn eighteen, your credit score is usually at zero. Not good. Not bad. But not there yet. There are ways to start building your credit before you turn eighteen, but that takes being under the watchful eye of a caring and responsible adult. So again, have money or a person in your life who is put together enough to do this for you.

I had neither of these things.

We are now coming into a day and age where my generation cannot do this for their children because the choices they've had in life have been difficult, a lot like mine. Getting a leg up is hard, especially on your own.

In 2005, the summer that I would turn nineteen, I had my job at Wendy's back—a solid first step. I would need a car because public transportation where I lived was lacking. I would need a better job to both make more money and hopefully be less stressed out at the only job I had ever really known. I wanted to be more than a fast-food employee, so I needed to see if I could get a job that was above that. And because my dreams had died and my opportunities were limited, I would try to get into hair school with Amanda Jane. Once I had all of that, the very last thing I wanted was to get my own place. Just a tiny apartment would be great.

These were not just bucket list items for my life. They felt like necessities. I needed something to work toward, or again, I would have to lean into what was my default and stay in the same place, with the same people, with the same pretty terrible life that I had and hated.

It would eventually suck the life out of me to stay in that situation.

What I should have done at that time was make an actual list of things I wanted to try to accomplish and even put them in order of what made sense to try to do first. As it was, however, I was in such a state of panic almost constantly, that I just dove headfirst into these things and tried to do them all at once. Not necessarily a mistake, but if Mom kicked me out of the house one more time and if Grandma didn't choose to stand by me, I would truly be homeless. I was an adult now, and I needed to take care of myself, and I had my best friend Amanda Jane by my side who was doing just that. In fact, she was getting married, moving into an apartment with her sweetheart, and starting a life with him. She was near graduating with her cosmetology license and would be able to start looking for a good job and working her way up in the world.

Amanda Jane was the type of person who made lists and stuck with them and did the research it took to make good decisions while saving her money. She plotted and planned her entire life. She is a person to look up to.

So I tried to be like Amanda Jane.

In a scrambled attempt to sort my life out, I applied for new jobs, began going to car dealerships to see if I could qualify for a crappy car with no credit, used Grandma Jane's car to go to the school that Amanda Jane was attending and talk about enrollment, and, last but not least, pop my head into apartment offices to see how much their apartments rented for and how much it would cost me.

A lot. It would cost me a lot.

This was an incredibly overwhelming process, which was compounded by the fact that at the end of every day, I had to come home to a mother who hated me and was falling deeper into her own addictions and mental health issues and an empty room at the end of the hall that stood as a reminder of everything our life had become and all that we had lost.

There were plenty of kids who had it much better than I did and were given opportunities whether they wanted them or not, and there were plenty of kids who, if given the chance to take it, would jump into my shoes in a heartbeat. I had it both bad and good because at least (there it is again) I had shelter, a job, a way to get to that job, and food in my belly.

At least.

It takes a lot of willpower and dedication to make it in this world, and now as I sit here writing this, it takes a lot more than that. Willpower used to be enough, and now it's not even close. If I had it bad then, kids today are struggling in ways I can't even imagine now.

To achieve what I needed to achieve, I would need support. Love. Connection. Hope. A will to live.

In the first six months of my nineteenth year of life, I would go from having nothing to having everything.

Whoa, that took a sharp turn.

I tried, really hard, to get everything on my mental bucket list. I got the car. A lemon, as they say, but it was a car. It would have to do. A lemon was all I qualified for, but I got it. With only my name on the piece of paper and the job at Wendy's backing me up. After that, I was able to get a new job, one that I proudly carried my high school diploma into after interviewing to prove that I had done the work to qualify. It was a customer service position for the United States Postal Service. As a side benefit—something I had not considered—because it was a government job, I was also given health benefits free of charge. Something that would come in handy over the next couple of years of my life. Before I did either of those things, I sat down in an office with the recruiter from the hair school to try to get in. I did not and would never qualify for hair school without a cosigner or money down the same way Amanda Jane had done it after saving her paychecks. The person who stepped in for me when no one else could, or would, was my big brother, Cody. He signed the paper and put his trust in me. He was someone who knew what it was like to work for the things you had in life. Similarly, no one had been there for him, and he wanted to see his little sister feel proud of herself.

Finally, I needed an apartment. A place to call my own.

On the first day of my new job, a boy walked in who was late to our training class. His name was Shawn Neibaur. He's my husband now of fourteen years. He didn't know what he was walking into that day, and the hardest truth about all of this is that if I could go back in time and change that, I would (I seem to say that a lot). I would save him from knowing a life with me and just keep going on my own, but I didn't. He walked in late and sat in the only available desk in the room, right next to me, and he became my friend. This beautiful man came into my life and became the support I didn't know I needed so desperately. His family swooped me in under their wings and changed my life. They were the family I had always wished for but had never had.

I had the car. I had the job. I had the enrollment to the school my best friend was going to, and now I had the man, who would soon propose to me and move in with me in an apartment that was close to both work and school, and a new family to marry into that would change my life.

This sounds like the end of the story, but it's far from it. It sounds like a Cinderella ending, and in so many ways, I felt just like that. Look at this horrible life I came from, and all it took was meeting my Prince Charming and letting him sweep me off my feet into a new life so I could put it all behind me.

Wouldn't that have been amazing?

But from the very beginning, my mother had her hand in everything that I did.

The reason that Shawn and I moved in together so quickly was because she had done it again: she had decided that I was not good enough to live under the same roof with her, and she "kicked me out" by emptying my room yet again, causing me rage and terrible emotions. But this time, this time I had an out.

"Okay, Mom, I'm not coming back."

Shawn wanted to save me from it. I wanted to let him. It all happened quickly because I needed to get away from her. Yes, I loved him, as much as a teenaged girl with no life experience can love someone. As much as a girl with emotional abuse in her past, and a desperate yearning for anyone to say those words to her, can.

I was broken and he deserved better, but so did I.

Chapter 20

The End

I'm thirty-three now. I've written a book capitalizing on my family's deaths. This is the life they left behind for me to have. This was all they could give me. This life. This awful, terrible, no-good life.

What would you change if you could rewind the tape? What would you say to the adults in your life if you had a chance for them to take you seriously?

Something I heard someone much older than I am say once, at one of those big family parties that my husband's family likes to have, was this: "Becoming an adult doesn't mean anything. It's not like I know what I'm doing now any better than I did then. We're all just making it up, and no one tells you that."

This came from someone I look up to immensely. Someone who seemingly has everything together, with clear direction, goals, and success under their belt. And still . . . still they say they're just making it up as they go. Those words really stuck with me. And now I'm telling you that.

Adults have no clue. We're just making it up as we go, same as you. It just becomes scarier the older you get because you feel like you're running out of time and options.

I'm thirty-three years old. I'll be thirty-four by the time this can be put into the hands of teenagers across the country. I'm in a scary situation because I quit my day job so that I could write full-time and dedicate myself to this thing called the opioid epidemic. I gave up making money so that I could connect with youth who have no one to connect with because money doesn't matter. People matter. And yet, people all over the world forget that people matter. Without people, what good is money? Money wouldn't exist. So much in our lives wouldn't exist. Opioids wouldn't exist. Now, it seems, we only exist for the sake of putting money in someone else's pocket. Or pills in someone's mouth.

I'll tell you how I do it—with the support of my husband. He agrees with me on all of this, and by supporting each other and our goals together, we are making this life work so that I can spread this message as far and wide as I can throw it. This is the kind of support that everyone needs. People to believe in them. He's the first person outside of Amanda Jane and Cody to believe that I'm capable of being more than what I was given in this life.

I read a lot of self-help books because emotionally I'm a broken person. So I want to find ways to be better. By the end of this book, I want to be able to give you some hope to lean on. Some light at the end of the dark tunnel. Something to look forward to.

Here's the thing, though, the thing that, again, no one wants to give you: we need a reality check. There is no real world that you're growing up to someday be part of. You're already living in it. There are days when your parents or guardians have no idea how they're going to pay the rent or mortgage or that bill for that injury you got while playing whatever sport, etc.

No one is happy. Happiness is a vague concept that we are all striving to reach, but it is fleeting, and it is not real. If you find it, it does not last but a few moments in time. Happiness should not be the end goal.

No one is sad either. If happiness doesn't exist in a tangible form, neither does sadness. Our emotions are entirely dependent on our physical bodies. This is something that blew my mind to think about, but maybe you're ahead of me on this one.

Emotions are just chemical reactions in our bodies. That's why there is no way to find the one thing that can give us that constant chemical to keep us bright and chipper. That's why drugs and other substances can screw up our mental stability so badly. It is causing differing chemical reactions. They are literally in charge of our emotions.

Joy or happiness is fleeting because the things that make those correct chemical changes in our bodies are also fleeting. Your emotions will bounce around all day, every day for the rest of your life.

This is all to say that unfortunately I can't give you a book with a fairy-tale ending. *D*mmit, Disney*. I can't wrap it up in a nice little package and say "the moral of the story is . . ." because there isn't one.

If you related to my story at all, then you need help. You need connection. You need support. You need it now, and you'll continue needing it throughout the rest of your life. The people around you will too.

Before I finish the book, let me tell you how the rest of them died. Let me tell you about this chain reaction of support and why it is so critical in our lives, now more than ever.

Chapter 21

Other Endings

I was married at the age of nineteen. I had my first baby at the age of twenty, and when I was twenty-one years old, on what was Amanda Jane's twenty-second birthday, June 15, 2008, Grandma Jane died. She had a stroke. She had lived a life full of depression and heart-ache after witnessing not just the death of her oldest daughter due to an accidental overdose, but also the death of her only son to suicide two years before her own death, while also being the caretaker to her second daughter, Diane, and her granddaughter, me.

Does Grandma Jane count as one of the many who died because of the opioid epidemic? No.

Was her life consumed by those drugs and what they did to our family? Yes.

The fallout is real, and statistics don't account for these things.

Grandma Jane had her own vices. She smoked daily, and that was likely the culprit behind her stroke and her death. Her death was a catalyst for my mother to fall apart even more, and to sit inside of the hospital room with her while watching Grandma Jane die was torture. Mom knew that no one would have pity on her and take her in. What would happen to her after Grandma's death? She didn't know, and I was terrified because I didn't know either. I had a baby girl now, and I would do anything to save her from the life that I had known. I was not going to come full circle and bring my mother into my home and care for her like a child. Had she really ever cared for me?

Mom and I struggled for years. She bounced from apartment to apartment, as friends or the church (the Mormons) took pity on her and tried to help her make it on her own. We lost Grandma's house to the bank, and Mom coasted on government checks due to disability. She became even more addicted to the drugs she was taking, but I didn't see it that way because I didn't know what to look for. I thought she was sick. I assumed it was the lupus, but she was not okay and getting worse as each day passed. We had a lot of hard moments, and it nearly tore my marriage and new family apart.

Eventually Mom would find herself without a home. The decisions she was making, while not in her right mind, led her to homelessness, and four years after Grandma Jane's death, in January 2012, Mom would die of a stroke as well. Someone would find her lying around somewhere making the same snoring noises Teresa had made eight years previously, call emergency services, and have her life-flighted to a hospital that could take better care of her. It wouldn't matter where she ended up, though. She died anyway. A blood clot burst in her brain. Why? Any number of reasons.

They all died of strokes. Only Teresa's death was ruled an accidental overdose. She was the only one counted among the thousands who die every year by opioids. Grandma's death was either old age or years of smoking. No account that her life was dramatically impacted by those drugs in our home and the people in our family who abused them. Mom died on the streets after suffering a stroke that might have been caused by her lupus, smoking, or the drugs. Maybe it was high blood pressure from all those things, maybe not. Her death is now and will forever be a mystery. I was twenty-five years old when Mom died and pregnant with my second child.

I was still living that normal life that everyone saw on the outside, but I was a complete mess on the inside. I was an angry mess of a person who hated everyone around her because no one understood the pain inside of me that felt so obvious but was invisible.

When I was thirty, I finally went to therapy. And I resented the therapist because now I had to pay someone to listen to me, but she changed my life and my perspective on the people around me. She changed what I knew about my mother and ultimately helped me heal enough to write a first book and now a second and connect with other humans in a way that isn't toxic but, in fact, beautiful and healing for everyone involved.

She helped me see that although I grew up thinking I knew what was happening in my family, I just didn't see it. I was sheltered from it.

#NotForAlyse

There were so many things left unsaid in my company, so many things left inside of the hearts of my loved ones—Mom, Teresa, Grandma Jane . . .

I will never know how my mom truly died that wintry day in January, but my therapist helped me see that as a result of the opioid epidemic, the pills floating through my home all of my life, and the choices doctors were making on behalf of their patients and their own best interests, that my mother one day felt driven to heroin. A street drug that is illegal everywhere. Heroin is another form of opioid. It is made from the very same thing that opioids prescribed by doctors are made from. Opiates. Seeds from plants. Plants that if ingested can reduce pain and cause a high inside of our brains because it blocks opioid receptors in our bodies.

There's a great big chance that the reason Mom was losing her mind for those last several years of her life was because of heroin. There's a very good chance that when Mom was homeless and unable to get her normal prescriptions filled, she instead used heroin and overdosed on it.

My mother was a junkie.

For how many years of my life? I don't know.

While she babysat her granddaughter while I finished getting my hair school license?

Before she had lupus? After? Does it matter?

When I was a teen? And she was being "committed" to a facility for reasons that were never explained to me?

I don't know. I don't know anything about my mother.

What I know is that I survived it. I survived a home full of drug addicts, who were addicted to pills prescribed by people you're supposed to trust, doctors, and being told that those pills would fix everything.

Everyone asks me now, how did I do it?

Guys, I don't know.

I'm so tired.

I've been driven to be different. What is that drive? I don't know if I can name it. I've certainly had my own addictions and escapes. As a teen, my escape was cutting myself. It was harmful, but it soothed a piece of me that I didn't know how else to fix. I lost myself in music, art, and writing. Writing, obviously, has been huge in my life. I highly encourage creative outlets because they are far less destructive than substance abuse or physical harm. But I did turn to drugs and alcohol. I smoked cigarettes for three solid years before I became pregnant and quit for my baby girl. While both in Job Corps and with what your parents would call "the wrong crowd" of people, I smoked weed. That's laughable in some states because many are now legalizing it. I live in Oregon now where it is legal, but in Utah, where I grew up, it is still not legal. Legality doesn't change it. I used it as an escape at a young age when I wasn't supposed to. I needed to be out of my mind because inside of my mind I was suffering a great deal.

Being drunk or high or buzzed on caffeine have been things in my life that take me out of my head, which is a very scary place to be when you feel isolated and alone in a world that feels abandoned and hopeless. When you feel neglected and worthless.

These were the things I was taught growing up. This was the example I was given to lessen the pain of my life, and I was given this example by more than the women in my life. It was given to me by society because we use pills or substances to escape, and I'm not just talking illegal or underaged substance abuse. Diet fads. Extreme exercise crazes. There's a whole side of my life that I haven't written about in this book, and that was my escape through extreme lifestyle changes. I used dieting to prove I was better than everyone around me and shut everyone out of my life. That was just as lonely of an experience as anything else I had ever gone through. Proof that we can use anything to hide our true selves and that in hiding we will not find answers to our pain.

Who am I now?

I am an adult who should be setting a good example for impressionable young people, but instead I'm writing a book that your parents don't want you reading.

#NotForTeens

Because I get it, and they get it.

If you relate to any of the words I've written, then you've already lived a life you shouldn't have had to face at such a young age. You're already wise beyond your years for the things you are witnessing and experiencing.

What you need now is someone who can give it to you straight. You need help. I needed help, and I didn't know where to even begin. I want to encourage you to start looking now. To find someone you can confide in. Not someone who will tell you what you should or shouldn't do with your time and your life, but someone who will be a good listener and point you in the right direction. Someone who will respect you enough to recognize that you're a human being living an individual life. You are not your parents. You are not your siblings. You are not the same as anyone around you.

You have choices to make, and I hope after reading this book that you can see that there are choices you didn't know existed and stand up for your right to live a quality life because you deserve that, and you deserve it before you turn eighteen.

You deserve to have the answers to the questions you don't know to ask.

You deserve it right now.

Chapter 22

It's All Wrong

I've had a breakthrough.

The actual ending of any book I write will always be the hardest part for me. In school we are taught beginning, middle, and end. Give a nice conclusion and wrap it all up together in a nice little package. Summarize the important takeaways and give a sense of hope or purpose.

I don't think I gave you hope or purpose yet. Maybe more than when you started reading this book—I mean, it is chock-full of things you should consider writing down and acting on.

Okay . . . good job, me. *pat on the back* Even if this is it, I've probably changed someone's life.

I can give myself the benefit of the doubt, I guess.

But it's not finished. Something is missing.

When I said there is no moral to the story, I lied to you. I was angry. I'm still hurting so much because this world just doesn't make any sense to me!

I want to throw my hands in the air and scream loud enough to crack the earth in half.

AAAAAAAAAAAAAaaaaaaaaaaaaaaaaaaahhhh-hhhhhhhhhhhhhhhhhhhh!!!!!!!!!!!

Would I bring my family back if I could?

Yeah, I would.

Will I ever want to?

No, and that is a different question altogether.

No, because I would be so scared of doing it all over again, but yes, because despite that I would do it again because I love them and miss them every day of my life, and just like I believe that I deserved better than the life I was handed, I believe they deserved so much better too.

I live in fear. You live in fear. It's the word I talked about way back at the beginning. We are driven by fear. It's a very human thing to do.

I'm afraid now that I'll screw this up at the end, and after you read it, I will have done more harm than good for your life.

The breakthrough I had doesn't seem like much. I sat for days trying to figure out the right ending to this book. I wrote a bunch of stuff that sounded profound and insightful, and I deleted it. It didn't fit; it didn't work. It was all wrong!

Aaaahhhhh . . . everything is all wrong!

But I think that's when it hit me. It is all wrong. Everything is wrong.

Your life is not okay, you're not okay . . . what can I give you? What can I do now? Now that you know my story and that my life is mostly normal now that I'm an adult, except that it isn't because I've given up on all of my dreams to make this my new dream because it's the only thing in my life I've ever known or that has ever made sense to me . . .

You're reading words written by a woman who needs to go back to therapy.

#FacePalm

I still need support. Daily.

So do you.

So does your family and probably every friend you've ever had.

I feel like a broken record, but support is everything. That chain reaction of support that we all need in our lives. If you don't receive the support you need, it may feel impossible to turn around and support someone else. That's why this is a whole-family movement. Your entire family needs support. Your mother, your father, your sisters and brothers, your aunts and uncles, your grandparents, your cousins . . . etc. You!

I believe that the biggest takeaway that I can give you after reading all of that is control. It was the one thing I never felt that I had. Everything always felt unstable, and with new drugs and new choices, new things were constantly coming up and catching us all by surprise. That surprise causes increased trauma. That increased trauma creates panic and panic never leads to good solutions.

How can I help you feel more in control of your situation?

What can I give to you to help you feel that if something surprising happens, you can handle it, and be okay?

An action plan!

I'm going to take a page out of Amanda Jane's book of life and create a plan for you. We are going to make a couple of lists and give you the control you deserve to have in your life. That will be at the very end of the book, but I'm going to ramble at you for just a moment longer.

In the case of the opioid epidemic and the pills we all take daily, sometimes for years, it all comes down to an attempt at solving our problems. We have been taught that drugs, prescription at least, are solutions. In the last decade or so, we have been able to recognize as a society that those drugs are causing more problems now than they are solving. Now that we are opening our eyes to this, there is quite a movement out there to figure out what the actual solution might be. If drugs aren't it, then what is?

The thing about drugs is that they are prescribed for a reason. Some people do legitimately need them to survive the daily grind of life. Some people are struggling with things that are very scary, and without those drugs, their lives might be cut short too early. There's a hard balance here between what addiction is and what is necessary for pain relief. The reason I write, though, is because the number of pills being handed out is far greater than the actual need to have them is.

I am disappointed in humanity that it has come to this nearly globalized attempt to peer pressure all of us into one form of drug or another. Peer pressure doesn't end when you become an adult. There are many forms of it, they are constant, and nearly everywhere you go in your life, there will be pressure on you to be a certain way or consume a certain product. I was lucky enough because I was a loner that I avoided a lot of school-aged peer pressure. Most of what I dealt with came from my own family, my own mother.

Here's one of my biggest problems, though: my family was trying. We were all trying to solve our problems and being handed these little pill-shaped solutions from trusted sources, and in return, as an almost pay-it-forward attitude, we were then handing it to members of our own family so that they too could be healed and taken care of.

Pills were the solution to every single problem we ever had. Is it any wonder that an impressionable young teenage girl, me, would also consider turning to them when she feels sad, lost, lonely, and confused? This goes well beyond peer pressure.

In looking back on all that I went through, that's the hardest realization for me to have. Despite the hardship and the abuse, it was all tied into the fact that we all wanted a better life. We were all trying to get the same thing. Happiness. Health. Control. Stability.

But in using substances to solve our problems, instead of leaning on one another for support or talking, we lost every piece of that happiness, health, control, and stability.

Now your generation is stuck in the chaos that previous generations have caused for you. You're stuck in the same loop, on the same default path of being just like them because it's all you know. That's not your fault.

I'm giving you this book so that you can see something different and take that control back into your hands. Not only do you deserve that for your own life, but the world needs you to have it too.

I read a lot these days. Usually it's articles about the opioid epidemic. I'm unusually obsessive over news I see that relates to the life I've had. In one such article, it talked about the number of children who are now in the care of foster homes or living with their grandparents as a direct result of the opioid epidemic. It's some ridiculously high number, and it's not getting better; it's getting worse. This news is so scary to me because it means that it worked. Everything society taught us, about using these substances to solve our problems, and marketing to multiple generations of people . . . it worked! These crazy people in power have their money now while we sit and lose the people we love and lose ourselves along with them.

There have also been the countless articles I've read about addicts overcoming their obstacles, but most have children, and I always ask myself, "Well, what happened to the kids in all of that?" Usually these stories are very heartwarming, addicts changing their lives, but now these kids will carry trauma around with them for the rest of their lives, and what are we doing about any of this? Allowing them to turn around and become addicted as well because they grow up never being able to wrap their minds around the lives they lead and what they witnessed in their families?

I'm the lucky one who got out of that horrible cycle, but so many people in my generation, my same age, are either addicted or dying because of these same examples. I should be one of them. I took the same pills. I used pills to solve my depression or suppress it rather. I was curious about all types of substances.

So what sets me apart? Why am I so different that I didn't become addicted? How did I escape, and why am I not dead?

There are many answers to that question.

The first person to hand me a narcotic was my own mother. It was a Lortab and made me feel really sick. The short story to this is that I don't know why she gave it to me. I was being emotional, and she either needed me out of the way or she legitimately thought it would calm me down. Either way, at the age of twelve or thirteen, it made me sick enough to never want to touch another pill like that again. I couldn't understand the fascination.

That first death in my family scared me so much. It scared me enough that after witnessing that death, and the continued deaths of my family members, I started refusing pain medication in hospital settings while going through painful situations.

I have always been a hopeful person. Weird, I know, but this piece of my personality has driven me to constantly believe that I'm capable of more than what I was given in this life. You can't accomplish much while you're high, and that's also a feeling I'm very aware of.

I'm a dreamer. A lot like that drive to be more, I dream a lot and am stuck in my head a lot. I didn't fall into peer pressure situations as often as some other people did because I was a loner and kept to myself. Silver linings here. I'm very susceptible to peer pressure, so I chose to see this as a good thing. If I were more outgoing, I maybe wouldn't have made it this far.

Good people. It has taken a lot of good people standing by me and believing in me and honestly being around me even when I was not in a good place to accept their presence in my life. The people who are there for you even when you're an angry, hurting person are the people you need to keep close to you always. The people in my life who have patience with me are the very same people who I trust enough to tell my problems to, and they always help me think outside of the box and find ways to move forward.

Self-worth. One thing Mom taught me at a very young age was that I'm worth something no matter who I'm standing next to. She taught me to see my own personal value, and that is something I've learned to hold onto tightly as an adult because I lost it as a teen.

It's not always easy to find support and community, but now I want to give you the tools you need to create that for yourself, and it's so simple, but it will make a huge impact on your life and the lives of those around you. Be the example and break that cycle of abuse and addiction.

#NotForTeens Five-Step Action Plan

When my son was an infant, he started having problems breathing. When he was three, he was finally diagnosed with asthma. There's a long story there, but the thing I want to share is that when his doctors finally figured it out and sat me down to calm my mind, they gave me an asthma action plan. In that plan, they had me write down, and keep somewhere safe, a plan of action to decide if what he's dealing with is asthma, how to control it, and whether to take extreme measures.

Now I want to do the same thing for you, and I could be fancy and make a cute chart or whatever, but I'm not a fancy kind of person. I like things straightforward and simple. There's a lot to remember in this life, so ... you get simple.

I'm going to do this in three parts to help you understand how you can do this yourself.

Part One: *What are the questions you need to ask?*

Part Two: *A definition of each question to help guide you to your own answers.*

Part Three: *A personal example if I were to have done this for myself as a young teenager.*

Let's begin.

Part One

You can fancy up these questions however you choose. You can write down your answers in the book if you have a paperback or write them down either in a notebook or an app on your phone. Maybe email or text them to yourself. Whichever way you decide to do this, here are the five main questions I've decided would be most helpful to you no matter what your situation might look like.

1. What is in your control?

2. Who can you talk to?

3. Who can you stay with?

4. When do you act?

5. How do you cope?

Part Two

Now that we know what questions to ask, let me help you decide how to best answer each one.

WHAT IS IN YOUR CONTROL?

Think about your situation. Remember that you are in control of your own body. Your own thoughts. You have more power in yourself than you realize. Steady yourself and think about the things you can do for yourself or for someone else. What do you have at your disposal? Think of things you have access to. Cars, phones, neighbors … etc. More answers might come to you after answering the next few questions. Also, turn off social media if it's becoming too much to handle. It's okay to put it down and not respond to any meanness happening online. This is the act of grounding yourself. Bringing awareness to the simplicity of being human and having control over your own breath and movement. Knowing that you are in control of who you are, and what you do, and no one else.

WHO CAN YOU TALK TO?

Start by writing a list of names. It might be a short list, and that's okay. Maybe it only has one name, but one name is really all you need to start with. The people on your list should be people you will be comfortable reaching out to. Once you've created your plan, I want you to reach out. Call, text, chat, app, letter … what is your preferred communication option?

Ask them this: if something happens in my life and I need someone to talk to about it, can I come to you?

Tell them as much or as little as you like. Tell them about your action plan, about the book you just read, and if you're comfortable, about something going on in your life and why this is important to you.

I know this one might sound intimidating, but this is a way for you to create the support and community you need, and you do need it.

WHO CAN YOU STAY WITH?

This is a lot like the last question, and the names you write here might match the names you wrote above. You may have fewer names here, but again, one is all that matters.

If something serious were to happen in your home, who would you be comfortable staying with for one or multiple days until your situation stabilized? Doing this will help you be more comfortable if something does come up, and you'll know that you always have a place to go.

WHEN DO YOU ACT?

This is tricky. I know. I've been there. It's difficult to know when to take your plan and put it into action. There are a few things to consider here:

Have you been hurt? In some serious cases, calling emergency services (911 in the United States) is the best thing to do. If anyone ever physically harms you, you have every right to make this phone call. Police and emergency crews are there for you, for this very reason. Please tell them you were hurt.

Has someone else been hurt? Or are they unable to wake up? Again, emergency services might be the best thing to do here if someone has been hurt or will not respond to you when you try to wake them up.

In both cases, this would be the time to call someone on your list as well.

Some less extreme cases would be if you are feeling alone or unsafe. Feeling sad, scared, or upset and unable to talk to the people around you.

Some examples if someone around you is doing any of the following: name-calling, sexual harassment, driving while taking narcotics/opioids or drinking alcohol, and irate behavior, which is if someone is yelling, screaming, throwing things, hitting anyone, acting as if unable to control their emotions, or being neglectful, if you're left alone a lot and for several hours or days at a time.

Peer Pressure

I just had my daughter read this, and she brought this to my attention.

Sometimes movies and TV make it look like we should keep things to ourselves when we are being peer pressured into something we don't feel comfortable doing. That is another situation in your life that you can consider talking to someone about.

Different situations might cause you to think of different people to talk to. I would have likely talked to Cody or Amanda Jane about peer pressure and talked to Grandma Jane about more serious things. I really should have, and that's my point. I didn't because I didn't realize I needed to, but now that you've read all of this, you know to do these things and not bottle up everything you're feeling.

HOW DO YOU COPE?

This is another list of things you enjoy doing that help you take your mind off of the stressful situation. Art, music, books, taking walks or exercising, writing, playing with a pet, calling a friend to hang out … etc. There's a lot that could be put down here. What do you enjoy doing? In some cases, I would even recommend finding a way to bring your hobby with you if you know you're going to be in a stressful situation.

Part Three

I want to show you what my answers would have looked like while I was going through the things I lived with in my family. Now that I'm an adult, I could even use the same plan to do that same thing. My answers might not even change. Let's see how this goes:

WHAT IS IN YOUR CONTROL?

Taking deep breaths.

Turning on some music.

Lying down on my bed.

Writing in my journal, being with my own thoughts.

WHO CAN YOU TALK TO?

(Put a check mark if you talked to them.)

Grandma Jane

Cody

Walk over to neighbor's house in an emergency (I had a couple of good neighbors who knew Grandma Jane and Mom and would have helped if I had known or thought to ask.)

Teachers at school or the people at the front desk (They are good people to talk to, and they often have resources for your area about who you can contact in some of these harder situations.)

WHO CAN I STAY WITH?

Cody

Aunt Sylvia (Amanda Jane's mom)

WHEN DO YOU ACT?

If Mom hits me or yells at me.

If someone is hurt or won't wake up.

If Teresa drives in a scary way.

If I feel alone, sad, scared, or upset.

HOW DO YOU COPE?

Painting (keep a bag with paper, pencils, and a small set of paints)

Reading (walk to the library)

Writing (poetry, journaling, write a story)

Music (keep headphones close by)

I hope this exercise helps you. It's simple but can be as complicated as you like. Maybe after reading the book there are more questions you want to add to your action plan to help you feel more in control of your situation. This can really be customized to you and what you're dealing with, and perhaps someone out there can think of a better way to frame this? In fact, I bet there are some people who can, and I would love to see what you guys come up with and hear your stories of reaching out to people in your lives to create your support system.

And take this slowly. No pressure to do it quickly. Adding just one person in your life who you can talk to and confide in is amazing, and I bet they tell you some stories that you don't know about to help you relate more to the people around you and feel less alone.

That is the beauty in connection.

After writing my first book, SO MANY people came forward to tell me how they related, and suddenly I felt like I had all of these really close friends who I had never connected with in this way before. It was amazing, and many of the connections I have now are so much stronger as a result of being open and honest about how I've been doing or by having these friends coming to me and sharing with me.

The last thing to consider is the other people around you. They likely need an action plan as well as their own support system. You can't control that for them, but if someone reached out to you for that support, please take it seriously and allow yourself to decide if you're capable of being that person for them. It's okay if you're not. Sometimes the best thing we can do for ourselves is to take care of ourselves. If you decide you can't be that for them, help them come up with a new person they can talk to or guide them to a neighbor or teacher who can help.

Small steps will make a big difference in your life.

YOU ARE NOT ALONE

Visit the Bottled Up Foundation at:
bottledupfoundation.org

and on Facebook at:
facebook.com/groups/bottledup